D1568297

White Sects AND BLACK MEN

White Sects

AND BLACK MEN

in the Recent South

David Edwin Harrell Jr.

Foreword by Edwin S. Gaustad

VANDERBILT UNIVERSITY PRESS
Nashville, 1971

COPYRIGHT © 1971
VANDERBILT UNIVERSITY PRESS

International Standard Book Number
0–8265–1171–6
Library of Congress Catalogue
Card Number 72–157742

Printed in the United States of America by
Kingsport Press, Inc., Kingsport, Tennessee

To Deedie

FOREWORD

THE old saw of logic, "All generalizations are invalid, including this one," has persuasive pertinence when one approaches the subject of religion in America. Caution is an appropriate virtue as one makes his approach. And after walking through that remarkable maze, modesty of conclusion and restraint in extrapolation are to be commended. Adhering closely to the path of scholarly virtue becomes a necessity in treating American religion—if one wishes his scholarship to be clearly distinguished from propaganda, if one wishes to be more the careful observer and less the instant expert. Of course, generalizations may come; presumably, however, they come only as did Bacon's "first approximations," to be further tested and refined.

The difficulties and treacheries in generalizing about American religion have existed from the beginning. Native Indians, colonial Pennsylvanians, western itinerants all saw to that. The twentieth century manages greatly to aggravate those earlier complexities: urban-rural, rich-poor, white-black, educated-illiterate, establishment-radical, hopeful-hopeless. Common goals, common sentiments, common codes of behavior are wisps that prove increasingly elusive. So, in the area of religion, we content ourselves with a pallid acknowledgment of a Protestant-Catholic-Jew categorization, hoping thereby somehow to encompass or at least to hint at the richness of Eastern Orthodoxy, the diversity of New Thought, the vigor of Mormonism, and the novelty of the Orient. That we do not even trouble ourselves about the omission of most religion with which this volume deals disturbs us not at all; in fact, the chances are that nobody will ever notice.

For in that trite trio of religious tags, the genus "Protestant" is the most misleading and indiscriminate label. What a strange assortment of battalions are asked to march under that banner! Or, on the other hand, what a strange selectivity generally limits the marching troops to a respectable, highly visible gathering from the ranks! For WASP does not really encompass all white, Anglo-Saxon Protestants; it points to those older American groups who have arrived socially and economically and whose Protestantism has often—in the course of this arriving—diminished or departed. In America of the 1970s, there are Protestants, large numbers of them, who happen to be both Anglo-Saxon and white, but whom none would think to describe in terms of WASP power structures. For these particular Protestants also happen to be as exploitable and as invisible as any of America's other dispossessed minorities.

Which is reason enough for the book before us. The virtue of Professor Harrell's innovative study is that it turns our attention to layers of American religion that lie below or beyond the level of most scholarly investigation. Here, in detailed fashion, the underside of American religion is held up for view in a light too often denied. An attendant virtue of this study is to show the "solid South" to be seething, shifting and re-aligning in its religious life as in so much else. If generalizations about religion in the nation have been regularly challenged, generalizations about religion in the South have rarely been complained against. The assertions have been all too flip, all too facile, all too pat; they will have less reason to be so now.

Institutional religion in our day has, as everyone beyond puberty surely knows, fallen upon hard times. A variety of crises, a plethora of challenges confront the churches and synagogues of the western world. Creeds collapse, traditions decay, clerical ranks dwindle, and extravagant structures stand idle or endure consci-entious scorn. Southern white sectarianism has its crises and challenges as well. It is instructive to note, how-ever, that these differ markedly from the crises that beseige the "Protestant-Catholic-Jew" syndrome of an accommodated Americanism.

The small Southern sects do not, for example, suffer from the much decried "suburban captivity." Cushioned pews and genteel respectability do not ensnare them. If theirs is a captivity, it is either of the hamlet at one end or of the ghetto at the other. Of course, one assumes with the author that we are really not talking about geographical location, but about socioeconomic po-sition. How much does class, as opposed to theology, shape attitudes, instill ideas, and mold behavior? Does the answer to that question change if the class itself enjoys scant prestige and affords little satisfaction?

If these sects do not succumb to suburbia, neither do they adopt the protective coloration of the culture as a whole. While the members of these groups may not know of Kierkegaard, they do know or at least sense the difference between Christianity and Christendom, between private epiphanies and public postures. Their temptation is not to embrace an American Shinto nor to baptize imperialistic policies, but it is to withdraw from all involvement that would take them beyond the constricting circle of the sect. Can that withdrawal reach the point where it becomes a sort of collective psychosis? Does the religious world view of the individual member become increasingly idiosyncratic and inescapably irrelevant?

Third, the institutional religion treated here does not suffer from that crisis of authority so familiar in the older, more visible churches. Authority is sure, and sure at almost any level. The revelation of God in scripture is firmly held, all of the learned analyses and apologies to the contrary notwithstanding. Also the hierarchy—too grand a term in most instances—is honored and obeyed, for the basis of the leadership's authority is repeatedly authenticated: God's grace is showered down, and charisma (real charisma, not the ersatz cliché variety) is the palpable result. And tradition too, for all its newness, exercises a powerful grip that few see any reason to challenge. Scripture, clergy, tradition —all continue to restrain, to discipline, to call for and receive obedience. What happens, however, when founders fail or die? Is the flexibility of first-generation charisma foreordained to turn into legalism and rigidity in a later day?

Finally, these groups are not confronted with a challenge in theology. Lippmann's "acids of modernity" of the 1920s have not, one-half century later, yet penetrated or dissolved the dogmatic containers of southern sectarianism. The historic warfare between science and religion is here fought on uneven ground: the victor is known before the first blood is drawn. A battle between sacred and profane is a mock battle, for all know that the earth is the Lord's and the fullness thereof. If denunciations of "modernism" are heard, the modernism being attacked is more likely to concern social habits or ecclesiastical innovations than it does major theological revisions. The severest theological disputations are not likely to occur in the name of Freud, Barth, Bultmann, or Altizer, but in the spirit of a scholasticism more congenial to an earlier age. What effect will enlarged educational opportunities for the clergy have on a theological evolution? More imminently, what effect will an educated youth have on a traditionalist clergy?

These crises of southern white sectarianism go largely unrecognized by Vatican II, largely unnoted in gatherings of the Consultation on Church Union. Crises of poverty, ignorance, shrill defensiveness, lonely irrelevance, emotional turbulence, and impotent futility are familiar concomitants of a minority status in American society. The redneck minority, in addition, rarely faces the problem of too much well-intentioned paternalism, rarely suffers from a surfeit of compassion. This minority has no voice in Congress, no membership in the President's cabinet, no token appointment in the judiciary. Its clergy do not participate in presidential inaugural ceremonies nor receive invitations to conduct White House Sunday services. Rednecks are America's real outcastes.

Yet the people whom Professor Harrell describes number about the same as America's Jewish population, number more than all Episcopalians in the nation, and number ten times America's Indian population. Invisibility can be color blind too. So if this is a day of collapsing stereotypes and rising social sensitivities, then we need to become better informed than we now are about southern sectarianism. This is especially true if our opportunities to become informed have been limited to the library and the classroom.

To begin the stereotypical deterioration, the author would have us note the surprising racial boldness of the small southern sect in comparison with the disappointing racial timidity of the large southern denomination. The Church of God (Jerusalem Acres), for example, has among its twenty or so congregations a casual mixture of black and white members and a similar blend at all levels of its professional ministry. The integration which this sect knows and practices is indigenous, thorough, and largely irrelevant to Supreme Court decisions and FEPC guidelines. Rather, it has something to do with theology. Following the assassination of Martin Luther King, the bishop of this modest church declared, "To the Christian who has enmity and animosity in his heart against the Negro, I have only one thing to say—he has not yet truly found the love of God as he should."

To help in rearranging one's long-held prejudices against southern sectarianism, the author has provided among other things an excellent and extensive bibliographical essay. An invaluable resource, it merits careful review. Much else is to be found in this volume, but of course not everything has been done, as David E. Harrell would be the first to acknowledge. His is a brief book, the subject is large. The focus on race provides an organizing center; yet, so restless and multifarious a conglomerate as southern sectarianism resists neat organization and steady outline. In this difficult area, we need more examination of the intricate relationship between theological convictions and socioeconomic considerations. We need careful delineations in our use of such terms as "cult," "sect," "radical," and even "redneck" itself in tracing these tricky currents in American religion. More explication is due the personality of the cultic leader, the waxing and waning popularity of the group, the spontaneity and improvisation in worship, the task of transmitting the form and spirit to a succeeding generation, and the "cure of souls" itself. But since it is Professor Harrell who alerts us to how much there is to be done, it can only be bad manners (at best) to complain that he does not serve the whole menu to us at once.

So, gentle reader, what do you know of the Church of God of Apostolic Faith? of the New Testament Holiness Church? of the Church of God of the Mountain Assembly, Inc.? Nothing, in all likelihood. Delay no longer. And after reading the entire book, you might even wish to seal your new awareness by entering a subscription to the *Pentecostal Free Will Baptist Messenger* whose publication office is in Dunn, North Carolina. For other titles, other addresses, and other perspectives, inquire within.

Edwin S. Gaustad

Riverside, California
March 1971

PREFACE

THIS is a study of the racial views of a segment of white southern Protestantism. The churches discussed are not widely known, and the people who make them up are among the least articulate of southerners. Some of their racial views are predictable and familiar; others are unusual and call for a new look at the structure of southern society.

A number of self-imposed limitations will be obvious to the reader of this brief book. This is not an institutional study of southern white sectarianism. Scholarly studies of most of the sects and cults discussed in this book do not exist. In the bibliographical essay I have discussed the available secondary and primary sources of information. A student interested in specific information about a group should consult that essay. My brief sketches of sects, cults, and individuals have been intended primarily to place the group or individual in a sociological category. In short, this is a study of types of religious expression in the South, rather than a history of the thought of religious groups.

Neither is theology a primary concern in this study. I have not systematically discussed the theology of any group. When southern sectarians used theological arguments to fortify racial views, I have reported them. But I have intended to prove that the racial views of southern religious spokesmen are primarily related to class values rather than theological presuppositions. Theology supplies a rhetoric for the expression of these views. I am not prepared to argue that theology has no influence on social action, but this study concentrates on the impact of other forces in the formation of social views.

Given these presuppositions and limitations, this study develops a number of themes: the existence of a diverse and large white sect-and-cult community in the South; the identification of these groups with the middle-class and lower-class segments of southern society; the support of traditional racial values by the more established sects of the region; and the existence of an atypical racial attitude and pattern of behavior among the more radical cults and sects in the South. The views of southern sect leaders range from the commonplace to the bizarre; they are rarely either equivocal or dull. The racial views expressed by white southern sect leaders since World War II have important interpretative implications for the student of American religion and the student of southern society.

The source material used in this study was collected in scattered locations. I am indebted particularly to the staffs of the following libraries for their helpfulness and kindness: Oral Roberts University, the Disciples of Christ Historical Society, the Baptist Historical Commission, David Lipscomb College, Florida College, Bethel College, Emory University, and the University of Georgia. Visits to church headquarters sometimes proved fruitful. Especially kind were the staffs of the headquarters of the Church of God, the Church of God of Prophecy, and the Church of God (Jerusalem Acres), all in Cleveland, Tennessee.

Two good friends were kind enough to read the entire manuscript: Professor Willard Gatewood of the University of Arkansas and Professor Warren Kimball of Rutgers University in Newark. Their criticism and encouragement were useful and stimulating. Miss Evelyn Levert, Secretary of the Department of History, University of Alabama in Birmingham, has been an invaluable aid in typing the manuscript and compiling the index.

Of course, the continuing enthusiasm of my wife Adelia Francis in support of my work is not only helpful but absolutely essential.

Finally, it seems appropriate to express my appreciation for the work of the productive scholars whose ideas have contributed to and supported my conclusions. Those to whom I am most indebted become obvious with the reading of the book. It seems to me that many scholars have caught glimpses of the central themes of this study; I hope this book will bring these scattered glimmers into focus. Generally, I think, scholars have not understood the racial behavior of radical southern sects, but their discoveries, honestly recorded, have been rays of light to one looking for confirmation of a conviction long held and newly discovered.

DAVID EDWIN HARRELL JR.
Birmingham, Alabama

CONTENTS

White Sects AND BLACK MEN

Chapter 1

RELIGIONS OF THE DISPOSSESSED

A SIZABLE portion of the American Christian community remains conservative, evangelical, or fundamentalist. *Time* magazine, in a recent report on the United States Congress on Evangelism, concluded that a "significant majority among 67 million U.S. Protestants" belong to the "theologically conservative" churches.[1] Such shocking popular assessments have appeared periodically in recent years. In 1958, Henry P. Van Dusen, President of Union Theological Seminary, in an article in *Life* magazine, described the conservative sects as the "third force in Christendom." Van Dusen reported that during the first half of the twentieth century sect-type religious groups had grown at a rate of over 600 per cent and that "traditional Christianity" had lost "many of its members to the third force." He labeled the numerical successes of the conservative groups "one of the most important facts of the Christian history of our times."[2] Such esti-

1. "U.S. Evangelicals: Moving Again," *Time*, XCV (September 19, 1969), 60.
2. "Third Force in Christendom," *Life*, XLIV (June 9, 1958), 113. See also, Martin E. Marty, "Sects and Cults," *Annals* of the American Academy of Political and Social Science, CCCXXXII (November 1960), 125–134.

mates of conservative success have been fed by the buoyant claims of the evangelical press, most notably *Christianity Today.* A poll conducted by the journal in 1957 indicated that "some 74 per cent of the Protestant ministers in the United States designated their theology as conservative or fundamentalist."[3]

Conservative claims to numerical dominance in American religious life have not gone unchallenged. In a recent article, respected historian William G. McLoughlin attacked the third-force concept and minimized the influence of conservative religion. McLoughlin discounted the numerical strength of "fringe sects"; they were simply "an annoyance and a scandal to the traditional churches in the United States." He judged that the growth of the radical sects did not represent a "significant new shift in the dynamics of a culture" nor was conservative religion "capable of significantly altering a culture." He concluded, "Few middle-class Americans need or want what the fringe sects have to offer."[4]

But such uncritical assaults have done little to blunt scholarly interest in conservative religious expression in the United States. While it is true that sectarian Christianity is not a new force in American history, it is an expression of a persistent historical stream that has long been important in the intellectual life

3. "Reflections on American Theology," *Christianity Today,* IX (January 1, 1965), 347. For a scholarly analysis of sectarian statistical success, see Benson Y. Landis, "Trends in Church Membership in the United States," *Annals* of the American Academy of Political and Social Science, CCCXXXII (November 1960), 1–8.

4. William G. McLoughlin and Robert N. Bellah, eds., *Religion in America* (Boston: Houghton Mifflin, 1968), pp. 52–53, 58.

of the nation. It also may be true that the sects offer
little promise of significantly altering a culture, and
yet, historically, radical sects have been less captives
of their culture than have the "traditional churches."
It is eminently true that few middle-class Americans
need or want what the fringe sects have to offer, but
serious scholars are interested in more than what
"middle-class Americans need or want." If conservative religion is not the all-consuming religious wave
of the future, as its promoters frequently boast, it is
the religious expression of a large and interesting
segment of American society. Most American scholars
have been fascinated by the popular appeal of the
sects; the vitality of the sects has long been a subject
of curiosity to more liberal religious leaders.[5]

Serious students of American religion have increasingly become concerned about the paucity of scholarly
study of the minor sects. Robert T. Handy recently
pointed out that "the story of Christianity in America
has been generally told too much from the viewpoint
of the 'main-line' denominations, without enough attention to the religious movements of various minority groups and of the 'disinherited' elements of the
population."[6] The reasons for this emphasis are clear.
Influential people are rarely members of sects; schol-

5. A number of concerned liberals have written articles investigating
sectarian success. See, for example, Horton Davies, Charles S. Braden,
and Charles W. Ranson, "Centrifugal Christian Sects," *Religion in
Life*, XXV (Summer 1956), 323–358.
6. Jerald C. Brauer, ed., *Reinterpretation in American Church History* (Chicago: University of Chicago Press, 1968), p. 92. In a recent
book edited by Leo Rosten, *A Guide to the Religions of America* (New
York: Simon and Schuster, 1955), eighteen churches are studied, but
not one of the groups discussed in this work is included.

ars are inclined to expend their limited energies in
the study of "important" persons and institutions.
Only recently has the common man become a fashion-
able subject for historians. But radical religious
groups have been ignored for a number of other reasons. Sectarian leaders are less articulate and have less
access to means of mass communication; they are simply less visible in American society. Source materials
are scattered and sometimes inaccessible. Few libraries collect the publications of such groups as the
Church of God of Prophecy. Religious movements
rarely take care to collect the source materials of their
past until they have moved beyond the radical sectarian stage of development. Finally, sophisticated scholars are generally interested in a religious heritage
which is pertinent to their past experience; few well-
trained scholars have a compelling personal interest
in sectarian religion. Except for a few of the more
bizarre cults, American radical religion has been very
inadequately studied by both historians and other
social scientists.

The major studies of recent southern religion have
suffered from a lack of information about radical religion. Most students of southern religion have confined
their investigations to "the major groups," Southern
Baptists, Methodists, and Presbyterians, with some
notice of Episcopalians and Congregationalists.[7] Of

7. See David M. Reimers, *White Protestantism and the Negro* (New
York: Oxford University Press, 1965); Samuel S. Hill Jr., *Southern
Churches in Crisis* (New York: Holt, Rinehart and Winston, 1967);
Kenneth K. Bailey, *Southern White Protestantism in the Twentieth
Century* (New York: Harper and Row, 1964). Reimers clearly explains

course, one could not contest the commanding importance of these major groups. The "success" of Southern Baptists and Methodists has "earned" for them a peculiar place of "responsibility" in southern religious life.[8] One must be careful, however, not to allow such prejudices to lead to an oversimplified view of "the Southern church."[9] Too often the rich religious diversity of the section has been overlooked. In fact, the religious expression of a sizable segment of the southern population has been ignored. This omission not only distorts the view of southern religion but also obscures the diversity within southern society.

Evangelical faith is nowhere more deeply rooted than in the South.[10] Even the traditional denominations of the section are strongly conservative. The Southern Baptist church, while harboring deep internal tensions, remains essentially conservative. It is generally recognized as the largest evangelical church in the nation.[11] But in spite of the conservative strains in all of the large southern churches, every major denomination in the section has within it moderate and liberal elements. The result is a tempered mixture. If Southern Baptists seem archaic and backward

---

the limitations of his study, p. viii. Of course, one should not criticize these fine studies for having limited objectives.

8. *Southern Churches in Crisis*, p. xvi.

9. *Ibid.*, pp. 20–39.

10. For an interesting regional survey, see Earl D. C. Brewer, "Religion and the Churches" in Thomas R. Ford, ed., *The Southern Appalachian Region* (Lexington: University of Kentucky Press, 1962). See also, David O. Moberg, *The Church as a Social Institution* (Englewood Cliffs, N.J.: Prentice-Hall, 1962), p. 34.

11. See "U.S. Evangelicals," *Time*, 58.

to one segment of the American religious community, to a portion of southern churchmen they are the most recent example of liberal apostasy. At most, the major denominations form only the outer crust of southern conservative religion; a colorful diversity of radical religion teems beneath the surface.

A large portion of southern Christianity has long fit into one of the two categories established by sociologists of religion to classify radical religion—sect and cult.[12] These radical groups have historically been the religious expression of the lower classes in America.[13] They appeal especially to the economically dispossessed, although recent sociological studies suggest that other types of "deprivation" may also produce sectarian bodies.[14]

One recent scholar describes a sect simply as "a religious group that rejects the social environment in which it exists."[15] But the general characterics of a sect may be outlined in more detail. David O. Moberg's description is typical: "It is relatively small, has abandoned attempts to win the whole world over

12. The literature on sociology of religion is vast. A brief discussion is included in the bibliography of this work. The variety of uses of the church-sect terminology is discussed in Moberg, *The Church as a Social Institution,* pp. 73–99.

13. The pioneering sociological study of American religion is H. Richard Niebuhr's, *The Social Sources of Denominationalism* (New York: Henry Holt and Company, 1929).

14. Charles Y. Glock, "The Role of Deprivation in the Origin and Evolution of Religious Groups," in Robert Lee and Martin E. Marty, eds., *Religion and Social Conflict* (New York: Oxford University Press, 1964), pp. 24–36.

15. Benton Johnson, "On Church and Sect," *American Sociological Review,* XXVIII (August 1963), 542.

to its doctrines, and is an elective body which one joins on the basis of religious experience. It often rejects an official clergy. . . . Frequent persecution reinforces its separatist and semi-ascetic attitude toward the world."[16] Sects emphasize "religious and ethical fervor, their beliefs stress primitive gospel teachings, and their practices emphasize the way of life of the early Christians."[17] The exclusionist feelings and Biblical emphasis of members of sects has recently been documented in a study by Rodney Stark and Charles Y. Glock.[18] The committed sectarian has a more substantial identification with his church than any other institution in his society.[19]

Of course, not all of the minor religious groups of the disinherited have all of the characteristics of a sect. Especially as the membership of a group comes to include more successful and socially stable people, it tends to assume the character of a "denomination" or "church." David Moberg asserts that a sect's "fervor tends to disappear by the second or third generation."[20] In his pioneering study, *Millhands and Preachers,* Liston Pope listed the changes that take place as a religious group changes from sect to denomination. Among the more important transitions noted by Pope

16. *The Church as a Social Institution,* pp. 78–79.

17. Elizabeth K. Nottingham, *Religion and Society* (Garden City, New York: Doubleday, 1954) , p. 63.

18. *American Piety: The Nature of Religious Commitment* (Berkeley: University of California Press, 1968) , pp. 57–80, 141–162.

19. See Russell R. Dynes, "The Consequences of Sectarianism for Social Participation," *Social Forces,* XXXV (May 1957) , 331–334.

20. *The Church as a Social Institution,* p. 79.

were: "From economic poverty *to* economic wealth,
as disclosed especially in the value of church property
and the salary paid to ministers"; *"From* renunciation of prevailing culture and social organization, or
indifference to it, *to* affirmation of prevailing culture
and social organization"; *"From* nonco-operation . . .
toward established religious institutions *to* co-operation with the established churches of the community";
"From a psychology of persecution *to* a psychology of
success and dominance"; *"From* voluntary, confes-
sional bases of membership *to* ritual or social prereq-
uisites only"; *"From* stress on a future in the next
world *to* primary interest in a future in this world";
"From adherence to strict Biblical standards . . . *to*
acceptance of general cultural standards as a practical
definition of religious obligation."[21]

Obviously, all religious groups do not make such a
simple and predictable transition. Some sects strongly
resist denominational tendencies. J. Milton Yinger
has suggested the need for a new category, "established sect," to include that type of sect which remains
distinctive and separate in spite of a growing denominational apparatus.[22] In a recent article, Charles Y.

21. Liston Pope, *Millhands and Preachers* (New Haven: Yale University Press, 1942) , pp. 122–123.

22. J. Milton Yinger, *Religion in the Struggle for Power* (Durham:
Duke University Press, 1957) , pp. 19–26, 219–227. See also, Moberg,
The Church as a Social Institution, pp. 77–78. Other older studies
which propose basic variations on the sect-church scheme are Joachim
Wach, *Types of Religious Experience: Christian and Non-Christian*
(Chicago: University of Chicago Press, 1951) , pp. 190–196; and J. Mil-
ton Yinger, *Religion, Society and the Individual* (New York: Macmil-

Glock argued that whether a sect dies, becomes a denomination, or remains a sect may depend upon the type of "deprivation" which spawned the group.[23]

It is also obvious that many religious groups are neither clearly "sects" or "denominations." As the membership of a group becomes more diverse, it assumes a mixed and contradictory nature. Upward social mobility by its members creates tensions within a sect. Successful people frequently leave sects and join more liberal religious groups.[24] But many remain; enough ultimately may remain to change the character of the group. At any given moment a religious group may be providing "churchlike" meaning for one individual and "sectlike" for another.[25] In American history such ambivalence has typically led to schism, but not until after a long period of tension.[26] Obviously, the major denominations of the South, and especially the Southern Baptists, now occupy this transitional hinterland. So do some of the sects studied in this work.

Equally important in the development of southern religion since World War II has been the success of

---

lan, 1957), pp. 147–155. For good analyses of the strengths and weaknesses of the sect-church typology, see Moberg, *The Church as a Social Institution*, pp. 89–90, 100–106; Stark and Glock, *American Piety*, p. 159; Bryan R. Wilson, "An Analysis of Sect Development," *American Sociological Review*, XXIV (February 1959), 3–15.

23. "The Role of Deprivation," pp. 24–36.

24. See Stark and Glock, *American Piety*, pp. 183–203.

25. See N. J. Demerath III, *Social Class in American Protestantism* (Chicago: Rand McNally, 1965), pp. 178–189.

26. See Niebuhr, *Social Sources of Denominationalism*.

radical cult-type religion.[27] The term "cult" describes
the loosely organized religious movements which make
up the radical fringe of Protestantism. "One does not
join a cult," writes Moberg, "but simply chooses to believe its teachings and follow its practices."[28] Within
such groups "authority is at a minimum"; supporters of
cults are frequently also members of more "conventional churches."[29] The cult's "goal is . . . purely
personal ecstatic experience, salvation, comfort, and
healing."[30] The thought of a cult generally centers
around "one particular aspect of Christian teaching,"
frequently a "more esoteric and mystical one."[31]

Charismatic leadership provides the cohesiveness
in most cults. "Cult leadership," writes one recent
sociologist, "is charismatic, informal, often precarious
and . . . sometimes corrupt."[32] The influence of a
cult leader is sometimes limited to one congregation,
although most such prophets are likely to make pre-
tentious claims. Frequently, however, cult leaders
make no attempt to establish an independent organization but rather develop a following within the
established churches. Independent revivalists and
"undenominational," "gospel tabernacle" type congregations have flourished in the South since World War

27. For an introduction to the use of the term "cult," see Howard
Becker, *Through Values to Social Interpretation* (Durham: Duke University Press, 1950) , pp. 114–118.
28. *The Church as a Social Institution,* p. 79.
29. Nottingham, *Religion and Society,* p. 64.
30. Moberg, *The Church as a Social Institution,* p. 79, 88.
31. Nottingham, *Religion and Society,* p. 64.
32. *Ibid.*

II, particularly among the dislocated urban poor.[33] In the South, as in other areas of the nation, the urban masses have proved fertile ground for cult-type religion.[34]

In short, the radical religious world of sects and cults includes a colorful variety of religious expressions. Some scholars have proposed recently that religious groups go through "life cycles," beginning as cult-type movements and ending as sophisticated and well-developed denominations.[35] A standardized "life cycle" obviously does not explain the religious history of every church, but it does outline the varieties of religious expression at any moment. In its earliest stage of "incipient organization" a cult or radical sect often exists only as a protest movement within a parental body. Characteristic of this stage of development is "the charismatic, authoritarian, prophetic leader."[36] This unstructured period is followed by a period of "formal organization." An independent

33. *Ibid.*
34. An interesting study of the success of cults and sects in the urban South is John B. Holt, "Holiness Religion: Cultural Shock and Social Reorganization," *American Sociological Review,* V (October 1940) , 740–747. In Liston Pope's study of Gaston county, North Carolina, the same pattern of sectarian success is revealed. The rural lower classes in Gaston county generally stayed in the older denominations, or were not religious; the uprooted mill workers often joined the new sects. See *Millhands and Preachers,* pp. 70–95. Of course, the rural lower classes unquestionably formed an evangelical element within the older churches and they were probably vulnerable to cult-type revivalists outside of their denomination. Pope did not attempt to study the six independent churches in Gastonia. See p. 128.
35. See Moberg, *The Church as a Social Institution,* pp. 118–124.
36. *Ibid.,* p. 119.

religious institution is founded and followers are asked to join the group. At this point the new church will emphasize its unique importance in God's work and will be critical and acrimonious in its dealings with other sects.[37] In the stage of "maximum efficiency" that follows, "leadership has a much less emotional emphasis and is dominated by statesmen." "Rational organization" replaces "charismatic leadership" and the group moves from a "despised sect" to a place of "near-equality with previously recognized denominations." This period is marked by a lessening of hostility toward others and the emergence of a more elaborate organizational structure.[38] Subsequent developments in the life cycle include an institutional period and a phase of disintegration, both of which are characteristic of fully developed denominations.[39]

But whatever transitions take place in the life of one group, radical religion is a persistent phenomenon. Some sects, through social mobility, force their way up the scale toward denominationalism; others prove to be too exotic to survive, but the religious creativity of the disinherited constantly creates new forms of radical religion.[40] The persistence of sectarian religion has been an important theme in American religious history; in southern religious history it may well have been the dominant one.

The recurrence of radical sectarian outbreaks and

---

37. *Ibid.*, pp. 119–120.

38. *Ibid.*, p. 120.

39. *Ibid.*, pp. 121–122.

40. See Pope, *Millhands and Preachers,* pp. 122–140; Russell R. Dynes, "Church-Sect Typology and Socio-Economic Status," *American Sociological Review,* XX (October 1955) , 555–560.

the sources of sectarian constancy have been the subject of considerable study.[41] Some have suggested that urbanization and other patterns of migration in recent years have produced a "cultural shock" that has helped spawn radical religion.[42] But obviously a variety of social conditions can produce the feelings of deprivation characteristic of the sectarian mind.[43] A society where traditional values are threatened, whatever the cause of the social disorganization may be, is a fertile ground for sectarianism. Radical religion may provide a cushion in times of rapid social change, but it has characteristically provided the same security for the disinherited and dissatisfied elements in all stages of social development. Moberg describes the enduring sources of religious radicalism: "When part of a population are on the economic, political, educational, religious, or social periphery of society, they are likely to establish sects which comprise their own society. They thus protect against real or imagined injustices experienced in other institutions."[44]

Theologically, radical sectarianism forms a kaleidoscopic pattern.[45] Efforts to classify the theology of radical religion range from the extremely simple to the

41. For a good survey, see Moberg, *The Church as a Social Institution*, pp. 106–118.

42. See Holt, "Holiness Religion," 740–747; Moberg, *The Church as a Social Institution*, p. 107; Glock, "The Role of Deprivation," pp. 24–36.

43. Glock, "The Role of Deprivation," pp. 24–36.

44. *The Church as a Social Institution*, p. 118; see pp. 458–460.

45. William G. McLoughlin's statement that the radical sects are "all pneumatocentric" is a startling misstatement of fact. *Religion in America*, p. 56. While many of the sects emphasize the "Holy Spirit," others almost totally ignore the subject.

elaborate. Gerhard Lenski divides sects simply into
those that emphasize "doctrinal orthodoxy" and those
concerned with "devotionalism."[46] Elmer T. Clark
has established a useful table of seven doctrinal emphases: pessimistic or adventist sects, perfectionist
or subjectivist sects, charismatic or pentecostal sects,
communistic sects, legalistic or objectivist sects, ego-
centric or new-thought sects, and esoteric or mystical
sects.[47] In fact, the doctrinal emphases among radical
religious groups span the range of Christian theology. What becomes apparent in a study of the social
thought of sects and cults is that the theology of the
group is relatively unimportant in predicting and
understanding the social views expressed. The sociological makeup of the group is crucially important.

46. *The Religious Factor* (rev. ed.; Garden City, New York: Doubleday, 1963), pp. 24–25.
47. *The Small Sects in America* (New York and Nashville: Abingdon-
Cokesbury Press, 1949). For some other classifications, see Moberg,
The Church as a Social Institution, pp. 92–98.

Chapter 2

SECTARIANISM IN THE RECENT SOUTH

ECTS and cults of every type have flourished in the South since World War II. Southern radical religion ranges from such orderly and large groups as the Churches of Christ, a part of the "conservative wing of the third force,"[1] to a nondescript assortment of independent revivalists and faith healers. This study treats the racial thought of all of the major southern sects. But, more important, it is based upon a sampling of the thought of a variety of types of radical religion in the South, from incipient cults to well-organized sects. While it would be very difficult to catalogue all of the independent religious movements of the section, and would add little new information to do so, a survey of the varieties of religious expression in the South reveals much about the racial attitudes of southerners. In fact, the variety of white southern racial thought can be fully appreciated only when one understands the complexity of and the class significance of southern sectarianism.

1. Henry P. Van Dusen, " 'Third Force' in Christendom," *Life*, XLIV (June 9, 1958), 120.

Of course, "southern sectarianism" is an artificial designation. Most American sects have members in the South; all of the larger churches with origins in the South have spread outside the section. But this study is confined to groups which originated in the section and which remain largely southern in membership. Cult-type leaders are even less sectional than are organized sects. With few exceptions, the cult leaders studied in this work live in the South; but their clientele is often national. A few prominent faith healers with headquarters outside of the South have been included because of the large following they have in the section and because of the prominence of the South in their evangelistic programs. In short, sectarianism is not a southern phenomenon, nor is southern sectarianism isolated from American religion in general. But this is a study of the views of those southerners attracted to radical religion.

Literature of the following sects has been used in this study: Churches of Christ, Primitive Baptists, National Association of Free Will Baptists, Regular Baptists, Cumberland Presbyterians, Assemblies of God, Church of God, Pentecostal Holiness church, Church of God of Prophecy, Church of God (Jerusalem Acres), Church of God of the Mountain Assembly, Inc., Emmanuel Holiness church, New Testament Holiness Church, Inc., Free Will Baptist Churches of the Pentecostal Faith, Pentecostal Fire-Baptized Holiness church, Pentecostal Church of God of America, Inc., Church of God of the Apostolic Faith, International Pentecostal Assemblies, Assemblies of the Lord Jesus Christ, the New Testament Holiness church, and the Jesus church. According to the *Yearbook of American Churches,* these groups have a membership of about 4,000,000, but six of the churches are not listed in the tables.[2]

A number of these groups, especially the small pentecostal churches, are the most elementary type of sectarian organization. The International Pentecostal Assemblies, the Church of God (Jerusalem Acres), the New Testament Holiness Church, Inc., the Free Will Baptist Churches of the Pentecostal Faith, the Church of God of the Apostolic Faith, and the Jesus church are all small pentecostal groups including at most a few congregations. Generally, each is united around a charismatic leader and a unique doctrinal theme. The International Pentecostal Assemblies is one congregation composed of the personal followers of John T. Reed, an Atlanta, Georgia, pentecostal evangelist. David Terrell, a Greenville, South Carolina, faith-healing revivalist is the founder and leader of the New Testament Holiness Church, Inc. Terrell's influence extends into several states, but his sect is in a tenuous early stage of development. The Free Will Baptist Churches of the Pentecostal Faith claim about 1,000 members, mostly in South Carolina. Since 1958 the church has published the *Free Will Baptist Advance* in Camden, South Carolina. The Church of God of the Apostolic Faith is the name adopted by a number of independent and conserva-

2. Lauris B. Whitman, ed., *Yearbook of American Churches* (New York: Council Press, 1969), pp. 170–182. See also, Frank S. Mead, *Handbook of Denominations* (5th ed., rev.; New York and Nashville: Abingdon Press, 1970), pp. 236–243.

tive pentecostal congregations in the Southwest. The
Jesus church, a unitarian, "Jesus only," pentecostal
group, is led by Sam E. Officer of Cleveland, Tennessee. He is supported by about ten small congregations
scattered throughout the South. The Assemblies of
the Lord Jesus Christ, another small "Jesus only"
group, is loosely organized around the *Apostolic Witness,* a journal published since 1952 in Myrtle, Mississippi. The Church of God (Jerusalem Acres) is
composed of about two dozen pentecostal churches
which in the mid-1950s separated themselves from
the Church of God of Prophecy. They are presided
over by Chief Bishop Marion Hall of Cleveland, Tennessee.[3]

Many of the other holiness and pentecostal churches
of the South are very small and remain in an early
stage of sectarian development; their future is at best
uncertain. The Congregational Holiness church, which,
in 1969 claimed 4,859 members, was founded in 1921 as
a result of a schism in the Pentecostal Holiness church.
Its membership is confined almost wholly to the states
of Georgia and South Carolina.[4] The Emmanuel Holiness church, an offspring of the Pentecostal Fire-Baptized Holiness church, was founded in 1953. The sect
claims 1,200 members, mostly in the Carolinas.[5] The
Church of God of the Mountain Assembly, Inc., resulted from another schism in the Church of God of

---

3. The only historical information to be found about most of the
minor sects is in their own publications. Consult the bibliography for
a listing of the most important publications of each group.
4. Whitman, *Yearbook of American Churches,* p. 178.
5. *Ibid.*

Prophecy. Its headquarters are in Jellico, Tennessee, and its membership is largely limited to that state. The Pentecostal Free Will Baptist church estimates its membership at 10,000.[6] Most of its members live in North Carolina and since 1947 the church's official publication, the *Pentecostal Free Will Baptist Messenger,* has been published in Dunn, North Carolina.

The largest of the southern sects which is clearly in an early stage of development is the Church of God of Prophecy. Even though it is a young sect, it has been a springboard for more radical pentecostal expressions. The church began in 1923 when the Church of God attempted to curb the powers of general overseer A. J. Tomlinson. Tomlinson was impeached and removed from his position, but a minority of the membership supported him in establishing the Church of God of Prophecy. After his death he was succeeded by his son, Milton A. Tomlinson.[7] By 1969 the Church of God of Prophecy claimed 43,441 members and boasted a well-developed institutional program. The Tomlinson charisma is still strong in the sect, but it has begun to move into a period of "formal organization."

The four largest pentecostal sects of the South have become relatively sedate and respectable. They are all less belligerent toward other churches, more sensitive about their relative position within American Protestantism, and organizationally are reaching a state of "maximum efficiency." The Pentecostal Holiness

6. *Ibid.,* p. 180.
7. *Ibid.,* p. 178.

church claims a membership of 67,027;[8] the Pentecostal Church of God in America, Inc. estimates 115,-000 members;[9] the Church of God, with headquarters in Cleveland, Tennessee, has 220,405 members;[10] and the Assemblies of God, the largest and least sectional of the pentecostal groups, claims 595,231 members.[11] Differing largely on questions of organization, the major pentecostal sects are very co-operative with one another; they quite consciously consider themselves a united force for pentecostalism.[12] In fact, the four churches identify themselves with the broader forces of evangelicalism in the country and are all members of the conservative National Association of Evangelicals, founded in 1942. The Assemblies of God are the largest single group in the association.[13]

Most of the numerous Baptist sects of the South are quite old. Several of them are little interested in missions and are representative of that type sect which remains insulated from the world and strongly resists

8. *Ibid.*, p. 174.

9. *Ibid.*, p. 180.

10. *Ibid.*, p. 178.

11. *Ibid.*, p. 170.

12. The best general studies of pentecostalism are Nils Bloch-Hoell, *The Pentecostal Movement* (Norway: Universitetsforlaget, 1964) ; John Thomas Nichol, *Pentecostalism* (New York: Harper and Row, 1966) ; and Claude Kendrick, *The Promise Fulfilled: A History of the Modern Pentecostal Movement* (Springfield, Missouri: Gospel Publishing House, 1961) . Consult the bibliography for a fuller discussion of the literature about the pentecostal churches.

13. For information on the National Association of Evangelicals, see Bruce L. Shelley, *Evangelicalism in America* (Grand Rapids, Michigan: Eerdmans, 1967) .

changing its sectarian status.[14] Typical is the Primitive
Baptist church which numbers about 72,000.[15] The
descendants of a strong anti-mission movement among
the Baptists of the early nineteenth century, the Prim-
itives trace their origin to North Carolina. Strongly
Calvinistic, other-worldly in outlook, and congregational in organization, the sect has changed little in a
century. Their stronghold remains the rural South,
and their attitudes are reminiscent of nineteenth-century agrarian sectarianism. The membership of the
group has steadily declined in recent years, largely
because the urbanization of the South has created a
cultural milieu inhospitable to the sect.[16]

The Regular Baptist church, a group which claims
17,186 members, mostly in the upper South, is closely
related to the Primitive Baptist church.[17] The church
is organized into loose associations, but most authority remains at the congregational level. Although the
sect is Arminian in theology, considerable theological
diversity is tolerated; each association adopts its own
confession of faith. The Regular Baptist church has
demonstrated a strong resistance to change and has
been declining in membership in recent years.[18]

The National Association of Free Will Baptists, the

14. Bryan R. Wilson, "An Analysis of Sect Development," *American
Sociological Review*, XXIV (February 1959), 3–15.
15. Mead, *Handbook of Denominations*, pp. 41–42.
16. *Ibid.* See also, Charles S. Braden, "The Sects," *Annals* of the
American Academy of Political and Social Science, CCLVI (March
1948), 56.
17. Mead, *Handbook of Denominations*, p. 42.
18. *Ibid.* See also, Braden, "The Sects," 56.

largest of the minor Baptist sects in the South, traces
its origins to the Arminian Baptists of the colonial
period. In 1969, the church reported a membership
of around 250,000.[19] The sect supports colleges in
Nashville, Tennessee, and in Mount Olive, North
Carolina; it is a growing and vigorous movement.[20]
The group is co-operative in spirit and has obviously
reached the status of a stable and efficient sect.

The Cumberland Presbyterian church is the only
minor sect in the South with presbyterian roots. Characteristically presbyterian in theology, the group at
present has no peculiar doctrinal positions that separate it from the Presbyterian Church, U.S.A. In 1969,
the church claimed a membership of 88,540.[21] The
Cumberland Presbyterian church was one of the new
sects to grow out of the great revival in the West at the
turn of the century, largely as a western protest against
educational requirements for the clergy. In the course
of the nineteenth century the problems that led to
the founding of the church disappeared, and in 1906
the group voted to unite with the Presbyterian Church
in the U.S.A. The most conservative element in the
body, however, refused to accept the merger and
maintained its independence as the Cumberland Presbyterian church. Since 1906, a considerable part of
the sect has again made a transition toward denomi-

19. Whitman, *Yearbook of American Churches*, p. 172.
20. See Mead, *Handbook of Denominations*, p. 37; Braden, "The
Sects," 56.
21. Whitman, *Yearbook of American Churches*, p. 171. The best
brief survey of Cumberland Presbyterian history is Thomas H. Campbell, *Good News on the Frontier* (Memphis: Frontier Press, 1965).

nationalism, causing marked internal tension. Conservative elements remain in the church, but the leadership has become quite responsible and statesmanlike.

The largest of the southern sects is the Churches of Christ, which in 1969 had an estimated membership of 2,350,000.[22] The Churches of Christ are the conservative offspring of the nineteenth-century "restoration movement" initiated by Alexander Campbell and Barton Stone. The religious census of 1906 recognized a division in that movement by listing separately the Disciples of Christ, the more liberal element which made up a majority of the group, and the Churches of Christ. Although the division was not entirely sectional, the Churches of Christ has been overwhelmingly a southern body from its beginning. Entirely congregational in organization, the church emphasizes the importance of strict adherence to New Testament authority, especially in identifying the "plan of salvation" and in "restoring the New Testament church." The sect has been best known for its doctrinal emphasis on the necessity of water baptism for salvation, the rejection of the use of instrumental music in worship services, and opposition to missionary societies.

Like the Cumberland Presbyterian church, the Churches of Christ has not remained a sociological or theological unit since 1906. The most progressive element of leadership in the group is approaching denominational status; on the other hand, the most con-

22. Whitman, *Yearbook of American Churches*, p. 178. For a discussion of the literature on the Churches of Christ see the bibliography.

servative element retains the characteristics of early sectarian development. A semiofficial network of journals and institutions has provided a skeleton for division within the movement. Scores of religious periodicals reflect the varying moods within the church and highlight the growing clash between conservatives, moderates, and a rising generation of liberals. One schism, the separating of the most conservative element of the church into its own fellowship, is already obvious and permanent. A second, between the "statesman" leaders of the moderate church and the more sophisticated denominational type, is clearly visible.[23] In short, the group encompasses virtually all types of organized sectarian expression.

The influence of radical religion in the South reaches far beyond the limits of organized sectarianism. Organized sects represent the more mature and mellow expression of radical religion. The most ardent religious displays are likely to take place outside of firm institutional restraints. Independent churches and loose associations of churches are a familiar part of the southern sectarian scene; they constitute an important part of the pattern of radical religion.

The largest and most important independent church movement in the South since World War II grew out of an exodus of churches out of the Southern Baptist Convention.[24] To many conservative Bap-

23. For a polemical treatment of this development, see David Edwin Harrell Jr., *Emergence of the "Church of Christ" Denomination* (Lufkin, Texas: Gospel Guardian Company, 1967).

24. For a brief sketch of the independent Baptist movement, see Ralph Lord Roy, *Apostles of Discord* (Boston: Beacon Press, 1953), pp. 350–358. See the bibliography for additional discussion.

tists in the South, the Southern Baptist church has become a symbol of denominational decadence. According to one conservative minister, the independent movement is a protest against "infidel teaching in schools and literature, breakdown of faith in the Bible, Socialism and New Morality."[25] The early leader of the movement was J. Frank Norris, influential minister from Ft. Worth, Texas, who officially bolted the Southern Baptist Convention in 1947. Norris's caustic newspaper, the *Fundamentalist,* had a great influence throughout the section. By 1950, his World Baptist Fellowship claimed "several hundred independent Baptist churches in North and South";[26] it has continued to flourish since Norris's death in 1952 under the leadership of Harvey Springer. The Baptist Bible Fellowship, a rival association of independent churches, has also been extremely successful. By 1960, the Fellowship claimed to represent more than 1,100 churches and "one million Americans."[27] The *Baptist Bible Tribune,* edited by Noel Smith in Springfield, Missouri, has a large circulation in the South.

Many of the independent Baptist churches of the postwar period have refused to unite with any of the loose fellowships that have emerged. It is impossible

25. John R. Rice, "More Baptist Churches Leaving Convention," *Sword of the Lord,* XXXVI (May 15, 1970), 1, 6. See also, "Negro Integrationist Speaks at Seminary," *Baptist Bible Tribune,* XI (May 12, 1961), 6.

26. Roy, *Apostles of Discord,* p. 356.

27. W. F. Askew, "Conference at Jacksonville Urges Inquiry," *Baptist Bible Tribune,* X (March 11, 1960), 5.

to assess accurately the strength of the independent
Baptist movement. Bob Jones Sr., patriarch educa-
tor of the independents, wrote in 1960, "Independent
Baptist churches are springing up all over the country."[28] Ten years later, editor John R. Rice reported
that "hundreds" of Baptist churches "will be leaving
and have left" the Southern Baptist Convention.[29]
Furthermore, the influence of the independent Baptist leaders reaches far beyond the bounds of their own
denomination. In 1960, Bob Jones University enrolled
students from "about a hundred different denominations," although a majority were Baptists.[30]

Scores of independent Baptists have published religious periodicals in the South since 1945. Many are
obscure and local in influence; others are extremely
successful throughout the sectarian South. Perhaps
the most influential is the *Sword of the Lord,* published by revivalist John R. Rice of Murfreesboro,
Tennessee. The masthead of Rice's paper proclaims,
"An Independent Christian Weekly, Standing for
the Verbal Inspiration of the Bible, the Deity of
Christ, His Blood Atonement, Salvation by Faith,
New Testament Soul Winning and the Premillen-
nial Return of Christ."[31] At the end of the decade of
the sixties, Rice's weekly had a circulation of more

28. "Shall President Take Orders from the Pope?" *Sword of the Lord,*
XXVI (May 20, 1960) , 1.
29. "Editor's Notes," *Sword of the Lord,* XXXVI (May 15, 1970) , 2.
30. "Shall President Take Orders from the Pope?" *Sword of the
Lord,* XXVI (May 20, 1960) , 1.
31. See *Sword of the Lord.*

than 120,000, and his weekly radio program was heard over 98 stations throughout the nation.[32]

The fragmentation of the Southern Baptists into loose associations and independent churches led by freelance evangelists and editors is the most important example of a common phenomenon. Loose associations of independent pentecostal churches, formed largely to promote mission work, abound throughout the South. Some of these fellowships are quite old; the Pisgah Home Movement, with headquarters in Pikeville, Tennessee, was founded in 1894 and has published an official monthly periodical since 1914. The International Apostolic and Missionary Association, Incorporated, of Lakeland, Florida, is controlled by the independent pentecostal minister C. G. Meyers. From 1938 to 1961, Meyers edited the *Apostolic Evangel,* a mission magazine, and operated a school for pentecostal ministers in Lakeland. He was supported by independent pentecostal churches throughout the South. A similar association, supported by "Jesus only" pentecostal groups, is the International Ministerial Association, Incorporated, of Houston, Texas. These associations are voluntary and extremely loose in organization; they are the only public voice of many small radical congregations. Sometimes an "association" may be only one church urging others to join it in its mission work. The Full Gospel Evangelistic Association of Katy, Texas, which since 1964 has published the *Full Gospel News,* is in fact, only one

32. "123,000 Last Week: Why Not 200,000?" *Sword of the Lord,* XXXVI (May 15, 1970), 1, 7.

pentecostal church. Some of the stronger independent
pentecostal churches issue publications with more
than local influence and solicit co-operation from
smaller congregations. The *Midnight Cry Messenger,*
published by the Bible Tabernacle of Southern Pines,
North Carolina, is typical of such ventures.[33]

Cult-type religious leaders, working outside the
framework of organized religious groups, have been
extremely influential in the South. One southern historian recently surmised that "it is doubtful that any
part of the nation offers so fruitful a field for the rov-
ing evangelist as does the South."[34] The charismatic
cult leaders of the section, whose appeal extends to
those in the traditional churches as well as members
of sects and the unchurched, have varied backgrounds
and theological approaches. Baptist revivalists such
as John R. Rice have a broad appeal to conservatives
in the section. Several editors and evangelists with
broad interdenominational appeal have backgrounds
in the conservative Christian church. J. A. Dennis,
self-proclaimed prophet and pentecostal advocate from
Austin, Texas, was a Christian church minister. Billy
James Hargis and A. B. McReynolds are conservative
Christian church preachers whose messages of God and
patriotism have gained them followings throughout the
sectarian South. The political motif in Hargis's Christian Crusade has become sufficiently dominant to cause

33. For a general discussion of such groups in Boston, see G. Norman
Eddy, "Store-Front Religion," *Religion in Life,* XXVIII (Winter 1958–
59), 68–85.

34. Thomas D. Clark, *The Emerging South* (2nd ed.; New York:
Oxford University Press, 1968), p. 254.

him to lose his tax-exempt status, but to a large number of southern sectarians he remains an important religious spokesman.[35] McReynolds's work is only slightly less political. His *Kiamichi Mission News* claims a circulation of 100,000, and his radio broadcast, "Pray for America," is heard over stations in 48 states.[36]

But without question, faith healers have been the most influential cult leaders in the South since World War II.[37] The faith healers are a diverse lot; some command fantastic financial empires, others work virtually alone; some work within well-defined limits of respectability and are officially or unofficially related to one or a number of organized sects, others are totally independent and work under their own code of ethics. Together they wield a great influence on southern radical religion and are supported by their followers in a remarkable style.

Obscure and transient faith healers with only local or regional reputations abound in the South. Typical is R. G. Hardy, minister of Faith Tabernacle in Baltimore, prophet and traveling faith healer. Since 1961, Hardy has edited a mimeographed monthly magazine, *Faith in Action*. Hardy and his followers are related to no organized religious group; in fact, he perceives only evil in the organized churches of the nation. His messages are bizarre, but his influence is

35. See "Hargis vs. Internal Revenue," *Christianity Today,* XI (March 21, 1967), 671.
36. *Kiamichi Mission News,* XXVII (December 1968), 2.
37. The only source of information about most of these cult leaders is the literature they publish. Consult the bibliography for a discussion of this material.

not small; he regularly receives invitations from independent pentecostal churches throughout the South
to conduct healing revivals.

Most of the faith healers of the South are less independent than Hardy and have their roots in a well-
defined movement. In the years after World War II,
the pentecostal churches of the South gave birth to a
group of charismatic healers and revivalists who made
dramatically successful use of giant tent revivals,
radio, and television. The early movement was given
some unity by the publication of the *Voice of Healing,* "a monthly inter-evangelical publication of the
Last-Day Sign-Gift Ministries," edited by Gordon
Lindsay and published by revivalist William Bran-
ham. Lindsay, a respected figure in the pentecostal
world, has maintained the journal largely as a center
for pentecostal mission work, but through the 1950s
it was a major promotional medium for aspiring
faith healers. Increasingly, the more successful revivalists established independent organizations with
publications and promotional programs of their own.

During the 1950s, the faith healers and revivalists
began to sift into a number of specific types. Some,
such as Lindsay, began to center their attention on
foreign missions and became much less visible on the
southern church scene. Others confined their healing
and revivals to a single sect. Typical of this type is
T. L. Lowery, a traveling evangelist who is an official
in the Church of God in Cleveland, Tennessee. Although T. L. Lowery Evangelistic Association, Incorporated, is an independent venture, Lowery's revivals are conducted in Churches of God and have the

approval of church leaders at the local and national level. Lowery's crusades retain much of the fervor and color of the more independent faith healers, but his operation is clearly more sedate and responsible than many others. Institutional affiliation clearly carries with it standards of propriety.

Of course, the most impressive success story of the post-World War II faith healers is that of Oral Roberts. Roberts, a minister in the Pentecostal Holiness church, began publishing a monthly magazine in 1946 and began his "public ministry" in 1947. For the next two decades Roberts blazed the trail of successful revivalism. In 1949, he established the Oral Roberts Foundation and quickly became the "most advertised and 'successful' evangelist and spiritual healer of our times."[38] By 1955, he employed an office staff of 155 and launched a dramatically successful television series. Beginning with a network of 95 stations, Roberts rapidly expanded until his "weekly shows" were broadcast by 147 television stations and 360 radio stations.[39] Roberts's spectacular success, his humble manner, his organizational skill, and his moderate claims helped him to retain the good will of the major pentecostal churches.

Most American religious leaders viewed the postwar outbreak of faith-healing revivalism with great alarm.

38. W. E. Mann, "What About Oral Roberts?" *Christian Century,* LXXIII (September 5, 1956), 1018–1019.

39. See "Deadline from God," *Time,* LXVI (July 11, 1955), 41–42; "Thrill of My Life," *Newsweek,* XLVI (October 24, 1955), 1104; "Frenzy of Faith in a Man's Touch," *Life,* LIII (August 3, 1962), 12–21; Oral Roberts, *Oral Roberts' Life Story* (Tulsa: no publisher, 1952).

The *Christian Century* labeled Oral Roberts a "Ringling press agent" and warned that "this Oral Roberts sort of thing . . . can do the cause of vital religion . . . . harm."[40] In 1956, the National Council of Churches of Christ, in an obvious slap at Roberts, "challenged the ethics of selling air time to healers."[41] Although Oral Roberts remained the main target of religious critics, most liberals obviously assumed that all such "religious quackery" was of the same cloth.[42]

But such estimates were premature; they unquestionably misjudged the subtle variables in character and emphasis among the faith healers. Roberts was always a responsible and reputable-type campaigner. From the beginning of his career, he drew much of his support from members of the traditional churches and refused to criticize any religious group. In the decade of the sixties, Roberts made a series of dramatic moves designed to improve his image. He diverted an enormous portion of his financial support to Oral Roberts University and became president of the new institution. He suspended his old television series and then, in 1969, began his new series with a surprisingly sophisticated format. And, in perhaps his most stunning move, Roberts in 1969 became a member of Tulsa's prestigious Boston Avenue Meth-

40. "Oklahoma Faith-Healer Draws a Following," *Christian Century,* LXXI (June 29, 1955) , 749–750.

41. "Travail of a Healer," *Newsweek,* XLVII (March 19, 1956) , 82.

42. See "Religious Quackery," *Time,* LXXIX (February 9, 1962) , 42; "A Failure of Faith in a Faith Healer," *Life,* XL (March 5, 1956) , 63–64.

odist Church.[43] No doubt Oral Roberts has changed since 1945; he has, in fact, changed faster than the Pentecostal Holiness church that produced him. On the other hand, as faith healers go, Oral Roberts has always been a moderate.

The flamboyant and erratic evangelists who preach the most radical religious message in the South are a different breed. They rarely court organized religious support, and they are frequently scathingly critical of all religious institutions. Classic cult leaders, these radical revivalists emphasize simple messages of healing and prophecy. The most successful have grandiose careers.

In the early 1950s, the most widely acclaimed radical faith healer was Jack Coe, an Assemblies of God evangelist. Coe's healing claims seemed bombastic even to many pentecostals, and his financial manipulations caused persistent difficulties with denominational officials. In a bitter feud in 1953, he was expelled from the ministry by the Assemblies of God. But this did little to hinder his career; his healing revivals continued to flourish. In 1956, Coe testified that he had earned $22,000 the previous year and that he had "built up holdings of $500,000 over the previous five years."[44] Coe's dramatic career came to a premature end in 1958 when he died of polio at the age of 38.

43. "Oral Roberts Joins the Methodists," *Christianity Today*, XII (April 12, 1968), 706.

44. "A Failure of Faith in a Faith Healer," *Life*, XL (March 5, 1956), 64; "Coe's Cure," *Newsweek*, XLVII (February 27, 1956), 47.

During the 1950s and 1960s, scores of other faith healers in the South made only slightly less spectacular reputations. LeRoy Jenkins of Tampa, Florida, and Gene Ewing of Dallas, Texas, reached large audiences with their radio and television programs. They issued typical monthly publications brandishing their healing miracles and promoting mission work.

But in the decade of the 1960s the most popular faith healer throughout the South was probably Asa A. Allen, whose headquarters were located in Miracle Valley, Arizona.[45] Allen, who died in June 1970, was a contemporary of Oral Roberts and Jack Coe in the healing movement of the late 1940s. The death of Coe and the moderate evolution of Roberts opened the door for Allen to become the foremost of the radical faith healers. His charismatic personality and melodramatic performances gained him a huge following in the South, which was probably his solidest stronghold.[46]

Radical religion is obviously a broad and far-reaching force in southern society. Furthermore, it is the voice of a segment of the society which has little access to other means of public expression. The southern sects are composed largely of the "economically and socially dispossessed," those who feel that the con-

45. For a sociological study of Allen's movement, see Howard Elinson, "The Implications of Pentecostal Religion for Intellectualism, Politics, and Race Relations," *American Journal of Sociology*, LXX (January 1965), 403–415.

46. *Ibid.*, 406. See also, "Allen Revival Hour International Radio and TV Network," *Miracle Magazine*, VII (November 1961), 8.

ventional churches are class institutions where a "lower class person cannot feel at home."[47] The sect or cult which he supports is likely to be the only institution which such a person controls. In their classic study of a southern community, the authors of *Deep South* found that lower-class southerners took "no part in the organizations and group activities of the other classes or of the community as a whole, and seemed but slightly interested."[48] The sect and cult leaders are the spokesmen of the inarticulate common man; they speak the mind of those who have no institutional means of public expression or those who silently exist in institutions controlled by men of quite different minds.

A study of the publications of radical religion can reveal as much about the social views of these inarticulate masses as about their religious ideas. The naïve assumption that sectarian leaders do not express social views is simply false. Historians have too long assumed that all sects "are essentially apolitical and withdrawn."[49] Whatever their theology may be, southern sectarian churchmen have rarely been totally silent about their social views.

47. See David O. Moberg, *The Church as a Social Institution* (Englewood Cliffs, N.J.: Prentice-Hall, 1962), p. 88.
48. Allison Davis, Burleigh B. Gardner and Mary R. Gardner, *Deep South* (6th ed.; Chicago: University of Chicago Press, 1949), p. 80. See also, Moberg, *The Church as a Social Institution,* pp. 83–84; N. J. Demerath III, *Social Class in American Protestantism* (Chicago: Rand McNally, 1965), pp. 8–9; Russell R. Dynes, "The Consequences of Sectarianism for Social Participation," *Social Forces,* XXXV (May 1957), 331–334.
49. William G. McLaughlin and Robert N. Bellah, eds., *Religion in America* (Boston: Houghton Mifflin, 1968), p. 57.

The theology of a sect may well influence the vigor of its social expression. One recent scholar has suggested that sects react to their society in three ways: "acceptance," "aggression," and "avoidance." Some sects accept "rather than challenge . . . the social pattern, because of their belief that personal sins and failings instead of an evil society are the key difficulties." Others exhibit an aggressive attitude "against an evil society and an accompanying program of social reform is emphasized." More common, however, is an attitude of avoidance "which involves devaluing the present life and world and projecting hopes into a future, perfect world." This type approach leads to an attitude of "indifference" about social evils.[50] Some sects include members who fit into each of the three categories; others are more unified in attitude.

But, whatever a sectarian may think of his theoretical responsibility to society, every religious man imposes his world view and social needs on his religious thought.[51] Social commentary may be a "manifest function" of a sect or it may be a "latent function," but it will rarely be totally absent.[52] The way a religious man views the world will generally find expression under a seal of sacred approval. Since World War II, southern sectarian leaders have left abundant tes-

50. J. Milton Yinger, ed., *Religion, Society and the Individual* (New York: Macmillan, 1957), pp. 147–155.
51. An interesting case study of this point is B. H. Kaplan, "Structure of Adaptive Sentiments in a Lower Class Religious Group in Appalachia," *Journal of Social Issues,* XXI (January 1965), 126–141.
52. For an explanation of this distinction, see Moberg, *The Church as a Social Institution,* pp. 127–131.

timony of their Christian view of race. To some the issue of race relations has been of momentous theological importance, to others it has been a matter for casual concern; but few have pursued their religious goals without occasional forays into social commentary.

Chapter 3

RACE AND RELIGION

URING the racial crisis in Little Rock, Arkansas, in 1957–8, the sectarian preachers of the city consistently exhibited a "sense of mission, of doing what they must."[1] The conservative ministers opposed the integration of Central High School with a "basic certainty and assurance" and "a feeling of unequivocal support from the Bible which the integrationist ministers fail to find for their position."[2] Armed with a deep faith and simplistic view of Biblical truth, sectarian preachers have frequently been among the most vocal supporters of segregation in the South since World War II.

Since reconstruction most southern sects and other American churches have separated their black congregations into independent denominations. Although the details of separation varied from denomination to denomination, white churches generally have succeeded in discarding "unwanted" black churches, frequently aided by a separatist spirit among blacks.[3] By 1948 only

1. Ernest Q. Campbell and Thomas F. Pettigrew, *Christians in Racial Crisis* (Washington, D.C.: Public Affairs Press, 1959), p. 54.
2. *Ibid.*, pp. 52–53.
3. Jerald C. Brauer, ed., *Reinterpretation in American Church History* (Chicago: University of Chicago Press, 1968), p. 95.

500,000 Negroes in the United States were affiliated
with predominantly white churches, and almost all of
these were isolated in segregated congregations.[4] Perhaps as few as 8,000 blacks worshipped with whites on
Sunday morning.[5] Twenty years later the situation remained essentially unchanged.[6]

During the early years of the pentecostal movement,
interracial meetings were common, but two of the
largest pentecostal sects, the Assemblies of God and
the Pentecostal Holiness church, and many of the
smaller pentecostal churches, have always been totally
white. In 1946, the editor of the *Pentecostal Holiness
Advocate* reported,

At the recent meeting of the General Board of Administra-
tion this question [racial integration] was seriously discussed by our leaders. . . . The Board's decision was to
take definite steps to help the colored people of the South
in whatever way we could. First of all, to work through
established colored churches of this faith . . . for that
seems to be the most practical way of reaching the South's
colored people.

The editor added, "As for opening the doors of our
church to colored people generally that has never
been either practical or necessary."[7] A reporter at
the General Council Meeting of the Assemblies of
God in 1969 noted that among the "4,700 ministers

4. Frank S. Loescher, *The Protestant Church and the Negro* (New
York: Association Press, 1948), pp. 76–77.
5. *Ibid.*
6. David Reimers, *White Protestantism and the Negro* (New York:
Oxford University Press, 1965), pp. 158–160.
7. G. H. Montgomery, "Christianity, The South and Race Agitation," *Pentecostal Holiness Advocate*, XXX (September 5, 1946), 4.

and delegates" present not a single "black face" was
to be seen.[8] In 1969, the leading weekly of the Assemblies of God advised that if a Negro were con-
verted by an Assemblies minister, he should be urged
to attend a "colored church in the community."[9]

Of the larger pentecostal churches, only the Church
of God has a black membership. Even so, black
churches have not "kept pace with the white work"
and the sect has never had more than a few thousand
Negro members.[10] In 1926, most of the black congregations in the Church of God were separated into a
Negro Assembly and were not reintroduced into the
General Assembly of the denomination until 1965.
The history of blacks within the sect has followed the
same path of segregation found in the older denominations.

The pentecostal sects have been quite active in
foreign mission work among blacks. In South Africa,
the Church of God claimed a large membership which
was divided at a ratio of 6½ blacks to one white.[11] But
this mission emphasis has had little influence on pen-

8. "Assemblies of God: Fair Skies at Dallas," *Christianity Today*,
XIII (September 26, 1969), 1149.

9. Faye Cox, "Interracial Witnessing," *Pentecostal Evangel*, No. 2855
(January 26, 1969), 5.

10. Charles W. Conn, *Like a Mighty Army* (Cleveland, Tennessee:
Church of God Publishing House, 1955), pp. 202–203. See also, *Minutes
of the 40th Annual Assembly of the Church of God* (Cleveland, Ten-
nessee: Church of God Publishing House, 1945); "Our Negro Work,"
Church of God Evangel, LIV (August 31, 1964), 11; Wade H. Horton,
"From the Office of the General Overseer," *Church of God Evangel*,
LV (July 26, 1965), 5.

11. M. G. McLuhan, "The Nonwhite Races of South Africa," *Church
of God Evangel*, LV (June 28, 1965), 16.

tecostal segregationist policy in the United States. Until very recently the Church of God listed white and
foreign ministers together in their annual minutes
but included in a special category "Colored bishops
in the U.S."[12] Pentecostal interest in African mission
work has obviously never been rooted in social concern; the Church of God had no difficulty in working
within the South African apartheid system.[13]

All of the southern sects with roots in one of the
major denominations are white churches. The small
number of blacks in the Cumberland Presbyterian
church were segregated in 1869 into the Colored
Cumberland Presbyterian church. Efforts to co-oper-
ate with the blacks have until very recently been spo-
radic and ineffective.[14] The Baptist sects, the holiness
bodies with roots in southern Methodism and the
independent Baptist movement are all totally white.
The Churches of Christ appeared more genuinely
interracial than any other major southern sect, though
only by comparison. Small Negro Churches of Christ
were scattered through the South in the years after
World War II. Nominally independent congregations
in a brotherhood of independent congregations, the
black churches were in fact controlled by the white
churches of the section under a system of spiritual and

12. *Minutes* of the 40th Assembly of the Church of God, p. 27.

13. R. Leonard Carroll, "The Church of God in South Africa in
American Perspective," *Church of God Evangel*, LIX (June 9, 1969),
4-7.

14. See Thomas H. Campbell, *Good News on the Frontier* (Memphis: Frontier Press, 1965), pp. 70-83; R. Douglas Brackenridge, *Voice
in the Wilderness* (San Antonio: Trinity University Press, 1969), pp.
90-93, 150-152.

financial paternalism. By the mid-1960s integrated meetings were still considered "unusual events" in the Churches of Christ,[15] segregated institutions were still being constructed,[16] and the most popular church periodical continued to print a regular column entitled "Among the Colored Brethren."[17] Until his death in 1968, Marshall Keeble, a black Nashville preacher, dominated the black Churches of Christ. Keeble's white supporters were generally satisfied to allow him to direct the meager co-ordinated activity which took place among "his people."[18]

In short, internal black membership has not been a significant factor in the life and thought of any of the white dominated southern sects. Many of the sects have no black members; none has a large black membership; until very recently, those sects with black members have segregated them officially or unofficially into satellite arrangements.

Under these circumstances, it is no surprise that the radical sects of the South had no part in formulating the liberal racial pronouncements of the national re-

15. "Desegregated Series Unfolding in Denver," Christian Chronicle, XIX (April 6, 1962), 1.

16. See "First Home for Negroes Is Opened," Christian Chronicle, XXIII (January 14, 1966), 1; "Southwest Workers Planning Negro Bible School to Prepare Preachers," Christian Chronicle, III (August 8, 1945), 8.

17. See the Gospel Advocate.

18. For some examples of this attitude toward Keeble, see Reda C. Goff, "Keeble Says His People Run to Gospel," Christian Chronicle, XXIV (March 17, 1967), 4; B. C. Goodpasture, "A Good Neighbor, Marshall Keeble," Gospel Advocate, XCVI (December 30, 1954), 986. A paternalistic attitude is frequently apparent in the "Among the Colored Brethren" column of the Gospel Advocate.

ligious councils of the postwar years.[19] In 1946, the Committee on Moral and Social Welfare of the Cumberland Presbyterian church passed resolutions on subjects ranging from "Protestant–Roman Catholic Marriages" to "Recreation," but the committee did not discuss race relations.[20] The study of Campbell and Pettigrew in Little Rock led them to the conclusion that sectarian preachers were the most racist force in southern religion. They wrote,

The twenty-four prosegregation pastors typically lead relatively small congregations with strongly fundamentalist orientations. Though not representative of the entire community, these churches serve an important section of the population. Only one is affiliated with the Southern Baptist Convention; the others are either independent or affiliated with splinter groups. Their members are chiefly semi-skilled and skilled workers. Two leading ministers in the group are active in the local Citizens Council. . . . None has joined the biracial Ministerial association."[21]

Such attitudes spring from the racial apathy and militant prejudice common in the post–World War II South; there was also much in the sectarian Christian tradition to encourage such reactions.

Many southern sectarian leaders remain deeply com-

19. For examples of the liberal statements of the National Council of Churches of Christ, see H. Shelton Smith, Robert T. Handy and Lefferts A. Loetscher, eds. *American Christianity* (2 vols.; New York: Scribners, 1960-1963), II, 542-549.
20. "Further Assembly Notes," *Cumberland Presbyterian,* CXVIII (July 4, 1946), 3.
21. Ernest Q. Campbell and Thomas F. Pettigrew, "Men and God in Racial Crisis," *Christian Century,* LXXV (June 4, 1958), 663.

mitted to an other-worldly version of the Christian message. While this theme is perhaps strongest in the Churches of Christ and the Primitive Baptists, it is conspicuously absent only among the independent Baptists.[22] This other-worldliness has been labeled the "overriding consideration" of the southern church,[23] but it is more a sectarian characteristic than a southern one. At any rate, the "social gospel" met a unified front of resistance from the southern sects. An Assemblies of God minister admonished in 1966 that "if Paul went to Watts or to Selma or to Montgomery," he would not be a "civil rights demonstrator"[24] but would simply "preach Christ and Him crucified."[24] A Churches of Christ critic of the "social gospel" sternly condemned those ministers who "plunge into the fray" to "take advantage of some free publicity."[25] "Let God's ministers . . . be reminded," summarized a Lubbock, Texas, Churches of Christ minister, "that the most important emphasis of the pulpit has always been and will always be until the Lord comes, the salvation of souls . . . and not primarily the improvement of material or political conditions."[26]

22. See David Edwin Harrell Jr., "The Social Gospel," (mimeographed lecture delivered at Florida College, Tampa, Florida, 1960); P. O. Revels Sr., "The Church in the World," Banner-Herald, LXXIII (March 1966), 6; The Discipline and General Rules of the Pentecostal Fire-Baptized Holiness Church (no publisher, 1961), p. 8.

23. Hill, Southern Churches in Crisis, pp. 76-84.

24. D. Leroy Sanders, "To Serve Is Still Enough," Pentecostal Evangel, No. 2720 (June 26, 1966), 2.

25. Alan E. Highers, "Churches and Politics," Gospel Advocate, CVIII (July 7, 1966), 418.

26. Dale Simpson, "Let Our Preachers Lead the World on a Real Freedom March," Firm Foundation, LXXXII (April 27, 1965), 266. For some other examples of this attitude, see R. L. Rex, "Preaching

The sectarian doctrine of separation from the world often was interpreted to mean that the church, as opposed to an individual, cannot become actively involved in social reform.[27] As late as 1969, the editor of the most widely circulated evangelical journal in the United States wrote, "The Church as Church has no mandate to get involved in the socio-political matters."[28] This concept was widely accepted by the southern sects; again the Churches of Christ probably supplied the most outspoken advocates of the idea. A member of the Churches of Christ from Nashville expressed the traditional position of that group: "The Lord's church is not a denomination; therefore, it doesn't have to make public statements as to where it stands on anything; politics and what not."[29] "The church had just as well take a position for or against flexible price supports or the highway bill," cautioned a Texas preacher, "as to take a position on segregation of the races in the public schools."[30] When confronted with the question of whether such a spiritual church

---

to the Mind of Our Day," *Pentecostal Holiness Advocate*, LI (December 1, 1967), 4–5; Irving E. Howard, "The Origins of the Social Gospel," *The Fundamentalist*, XXVIII (May 30, 1952), 4–5; I. W. Rogers, "Does the Great Commission Include the Social Gospel," *Baptist Challenge*, VIII (February 1968), 1, 4.

27. Samuel S. Hill points out the pervasiveness of this idea in southern churches, *Southern Churches in Crisis* (New York: Holt, Rinehart and Winston, 1967), pp. 105–115.

28. "Christian Social Action," *Christianity Today*, XIII (March 14, 1969), 544.

29. A Christian, "Nashville Reader Says 'Letters Were Ugly,'" *Christian Chronicle*, XXI (December 13, 1963), 3.

30. Ross W. Dye, "What Does the Church of Christ Teach on Segregation?" *Firm Foundation*, LXXIII (April 3, 1956), 213.

was "relevant," a Borger, Texas, minister replied that the Churches of Christ was not relevant as "some kind of rehabilitation center, civil rights correction office, or 'heavenly peace corps' " but that it was relevant as " 'the pillar and ground of the truth.' "[31]

The conviction that churches should not make declarations on social issues was not confined to the Churches of Christ. Warnings on the subject were common in pentecostal journals,[32] and even independent Baptist leaders, who are generally outspoken political activists, frequently made a sharp distinction between individual and church social action.[33] The sects frequently exhibited an ironic lack of consistency on this point. Campbell and Pettigrew observed this in their study of Little Rock: "Frequently ministers who at one point in the interview had told us of their sermons or lectures in defense of segregation, at another point would tell us that they kept 'politics and such subjects' out of their sermons."[34]

Another corollary of sectarian other-worldliness is the view that Christians should suffer wrong rather

31. Charles A. Whitmire, "The Church Is Not 'Relevant'—Or Is it?" *Firm Foundation*, LXXXIV (October 17, 1967), 662. See also, Clint Springer, "Unrest in U.S. Churches," *Gospel Guardian*, XVIII (April 6, 1967), 12–13.

32. For some examples, see J. Robert Ashcroft, "God and Government," *Pentecostal Evangel*, No. 2838 (September 29, 1968), 10–11; [A. M. Long], "A Vital Church—Concerned, Committed Conquering," *Pentecostal Holiness Advocate*, LIII (May 10, 1969), 3, 12; James L. Cox, "Father Forgive Them," *Gospel Herald*, XXVI (October 1966), 3, 10.

33. See Ernest Q. Campbell and Thomas F. Pettigrew, *Christians in Racial Crisis* (Washington, D.C.: Public Affairs Press, 1959), p. 45.

34. *Ibid.*, p. 179.

than protest against social injustice. A sense of suffering has been a persistent theme in southern religion; in such groups as the Churches of Christ and Primitive Baptists, it is a dominant doctrine. In 1964, a North Carolina Primitive Baptist editor advised, "Whatever government God's people live under, they must submit to its laws—good or bad, except they violate conscience. . . . If they happen to live under unjust and wicked rulers, they must still submit."[35] Another Primitive Baptist writer exhorted, "No man can preach the kingdom of God and contentment that pacifies the souls of men, and also be an agitator of strife and discontentment about his worldly rights."[36] The editor of the *Firm Foundation,* a Churches of Christ weekly published in Austin, Texas, urged Negroes to "carry the burden of life cheerfully." While the "social condition" of blacks in the United States was not ideal, wrote the editor, "it is far superior to that endured by Christ, and the apostles." He asked: "Yet where do you find any of these holy men complaining of their lot and developing within themselves a chronic discontent?"[37] Perhaps the most colorful counsel to be patient was a Negro folk doggerel printed in a Kentucky holiness paper, the *Pentecostal Herald:*

35. W. J. Berry, "Where Is Our Citizenship?" *Old Faith Contender,* XLII (March 1964), 69. See also, Stanley J. Duce, "The Attitude and Conduct of Believers in the Face of Growing Lawlessness," *Old Faith Contender,* XLVIII (February 1969), 50–52.

36. "Do No Violence and Be Satisfied with Your Wages," *Old Faith Contender,* XLVI (September 1968), 264.

37. G. H. P. Showalter, "The Sin of Discontent," *Firm Foundation,* LXXI (June 8, 1954), 9.

To eat with the white folks
We'll not try in vain,

And we'll all ride together
In the same Pullman train.

There'll be no distinction there,
There'll be no distinction there,
For the Lord is the light,
And the Lord is right,
And we'll all be white in the heavenly light,
There'll be no distinction there.[38]

The necessity of Christian suffering seemed to many southerners to bolster the argument in favor of slow evolutionary racial reform in the South. Even those sectarians who were political activists believed that Christians should suffer injustice and seek slow and peaceful reforms. The Christian would never anticipate that social wrongs would be "solved in a day."[39] In 1968, Tom Graham, Cumberland Presbyterian minister in Jackson, Mississippi, warned that "wrongs are not instantaneously righted" and, whatever the circumstances, Christians could only resort to "lawful channels for redressing the wrongs committed."[40] Sectarian leaders repeatedly argued that racial problems could not be solved by forced reforms but only when the

38. "Question Bureau," *Pentecostal Herald*, LXV (September 1, 1954) , 16.

39. L. R. Wilson, "Subversive Organizations," *Voice of Freedom*, VIII (May 1960) , 68.

40. "Are Riots Christian?" *Cumberland Presbyterian*, CXL (June 4, 1968) , 12. See also, Ky Curry, "A Sane Race Relations Program," *Cumberland Presbyterian*, CXIX (September 18, 1947) , 3.

question was "resolved in the hearts of the people."[41]
Holiness editor John H. Paul, in an article entitled "If
I Were a Colored Man," concluded that he would not
"deplore my lot" but would be "patient" with those
"who did not respect me."[42] Patience was extolled as
the Christian solution to southern racial difficulties.
During the 1952 presidential campaign, a delighted
J. Frank Norris published in *The Fundamentalist* his
impression of a personal interview granted him by
Dwight D. Eisenhower. Eisenhower, reported Norris,
was an advocate of the "gradual theory of . . . Booker
T. Washington" who recognized the futility of "quick
and violent reforms."[43] During the 1950s, southern
sectarian clergymen repeatedly warned the Supreme
Court that integration should be allowed to "evolve
naturally" rather than be forced on the South by
"federal law."[44]

In the minds of many southern sectarian preachers
the preservation of southern customs was perfectly
consistent with Christian principles. In 1966, Rex
Turner, president of Alabama Christian College, a
Churches of Christ college in Montgomery, suggested
that Christian love did not demand the changing of
"family customs, or national characteristics, or social

41. Donald S. Aultman, "Into the World, Not Out of the World,"
Church of God Evangel, LIV (July 6, 1964), 12.

42. *Pentecostal Herald,* XLVI (July 27, 1955), 3. See also, John R.
Rice, *Negro and White* (Murfreesboro, Tennessee: Sword of the Lord
Publishers, 1956), pp. 7–9.

43. "Eisenhower's Platform—God, Home, and Mother," *The Fundamentalist,* XXIX (August 8, 1952), 3.

44. "Question Bureau," *Pentecostal Herald,* XLIV (April 15, 1953),
16.

differences." "Such differences," argued Turner, "will always exist."[45] Segregation did no harm to blacks, the custom should be preserved. Elder J. Walter Hendricks, editor of the Primitive Baptist *Banner Herald,* wrote, "It is no injustice to a black man if a white man does not care to associate with him. . . . It is no mark of inferiority to keep the races separate. They ought not to desire to mix."[46] G. H. Montgomery, influential editor in the Pentecostal Holiness church, staunchly defended the segregationist policy of his sect but insisted that the policy did not "indicate prejudice, but expediency."[47]

Southern sectarian preachers repeatedly pointed out that Negroes were contented with their social position, an argument as old as race relations in the South.[48] "I am convinced," wrote a Churches of Christ minister from Ft. Worth, Texas, in 1963, "that the Negroes do not wish to have mixed audiences; they are more comfortable and satisfied to have their own congregations."[49] Many southern Christians sincerely believed that blacks preferred religious and social segregation;

45. "Christianity and the Races," *Gospel Advocate,* CVIII (May 12, 1966), 293.

46. "Some Thoughts on Segregation, *Banner-Herald,* LXIII (May 1956), 6.

47. "Christianity, the South and Race Agitation," *Pentecostal Holiness Advocate,* XXX (September 5, 1946), 4.

48. Most of these arguments have long traditions in southern thought. See John Dollard, *Caste and Class in a Southern Town* (New Haven: Yale University Press, 1937), pp. 383–384; Campbell and Pettigrew, *Christians in Racial Crisis,* p. 49.

49. W. S. Willis, "Preacher Says Negroes Prefer Segregated Worship Services," *Christian Chronicle,* XXI (October 18, 1963), 5.

sectarian periodicals frequently published articles written by southern Negroes defending the system.[50] Even political discrimination was defended. In 1965, a pentecostal evangelist wrote, "If they [blacks] were wanting to vote so badly, the constitution assured them the privilege. Anyone who has bothered to learn the truth knows that the average Negro in the South did not care to vote. Politics was a foreign concern to him,"[51] In short, the system of racial discrimination in the South was perfectly acceptable to both races. If blacks wanted to change their circumstances, they would be able to do so. Churches of Christ editor L. R. Wilson assured southern Negroes, "There has never been a time in the history of the nation when one who had the will to succeed, who played the game of life according to the rules, and whose character was unassailable, could not succeed. It has been harder for some. . . . How can it be otherwise?"[52]

Southern sect leaders have been particularly sensitive to attacks from the North. In 1949, the editor of the *Church of God Evangel* clearly sounded the southern view:

The South is the only section of the country that is capable of dealing with this particular race question, and if outsiders will keep their noses out of our business down here, we, the white and the colored people, will solve this prob-

50. See, for example, "The Southern Negro," *Brother Mac's Weekly Report,* no volume (October 14, 1968), 1.

51. J. Royce Thomason, "On the World and National Scene, *Voice in the Wilderness,* no volume (April 1965), 3.

52. "Who Is to Blame?" *Voice of Freedom,* XV (December 1967), 185.

lem to the satisfaction of the South, and that, by all means, should be satisfactory to everybody else.[53]

In 1946, after a racial incident in Columbia, Tennessee, the editor of the *Cumberland Presbyterian* bemoaned the "unfair" analysis of the affair by "theorists and legalists from outside the local section." While he agreed that "local citizens may not always deal out justice," he insisted that "just plain, common 'horse sense' and a 'good dose of religion' " would settle racial problems throughout the South.[54]

Southern resentment of northern liberal interference reached new dimensions during the civil rights struggles of the 1960s. When Bob Jones University was attacked by a northern Baptist paper because of its segregationist policies, independent Baptist leaders blasted back.[55] Revivalist John R. Rice wrote,

All you left-wingers, socialists, religious unbelievers and liberals, why don't you send delegates . . . to march on Chicago and Cleveland and Los Angeles? Why only abuse and law breaking and slander for white people in Mississippi and Arkansas and Alabama? We in the deep South are so old fashioned most of us still believe in the Bible. . . . We generally are against socialism and communism and modernism, and so left wing newsmen and modern preachers love to deride the South.[56]

53. "Editor's Note," *Church of God Evangel*, XXXIX (January 8, 1949) , 13.
54. [Ky Curry], "That Race Problem Again," *Cumberland Presbyterian*, CXVIII (March 14, 1946) , 3.
55. "Yes, Baptist Standard, Do Look Who Opposes," *Sword of the Lord*, XXXII (May 20, 1966) , 9.
56. "Editor's Notes," *Sword of the Lord*, XXXII (August 19, 1966) , 1, 3.

Equally furious was the reaction when comedian Jerry Lewis announced on television that he had "fulfilled a lifelong ambition" when he recently "purposely used the toilet in the airplane" over Mississippi. A Florida conservative demanded that "the Jew" immediately retract this "impolite and vulgar" insult.[57] In the minds of some southern preachers the remark of the "half-witted, loud-mouthed so-called comedian" was simply another "flagrant example of the vulgar, filthy, defamation of the white people of the South" which had become typical of the country.[58] One preacher concluded, "It is time for white Southerns [sic] to rise up and let the world know they will take it no longer!"[59] Such indignities from outside the section, warned another preacher, could ultimately "destroy the feeling of real love many people have had for the Negro race."[60]

The profession of affection for Negroes is an ancient theme in the mind of the southern white. Samuel S. Hill Jr. argues that the claim is a sincere one: "The Southern white who says he has genuine affection for

57. *Brother Mac's Weekly Report,* no volume (July 21, 1969) , 2.
58. "Southerns [sic] Arise!" *Brother Mac's Weekly Report,* no volume (October 27, 1969) , 1.
59. *Ibid.*
60. L. E. White, "Ridiculous Coercion by CORE and Others," *Christian Crusade,* XVI (October 1964) , 5. See also, [G. H. Montgomery], "Ku Klux Klan in the News Again," *Pentecostal Holiness Advocate,* XXX (September 19, 1946) , 3, 9; Joe Morrow, "Negro Issue Is Social Question," *Christian Chronicle,* XXI (December 13, 1963) , 3; "Character and Integration," *Baptist Faith and Mission,* IX (December 1964) , 1; E. D. Henderson, *God Save Our Country* (Cnatril [sic], Iowa: no. pub., n. d.) , pp. 5–6.

the Negro means what he says, and is accurate, *in terms of his particular definition of affection where Negro-white relations are involved.*"[61] However that may be, the argument is persistent among the religious conservatives of the section. J. Frank Norris expressed the sentiment well in 1952:

Well, I'm for the Negro. I'm the best friend they've got. I have several employed and they're mighty good friends of mine. . . . I like Negroes. I like them. But I am not in favor of them coming into my home and sitting down with my family, and marrying my daughter.[62]

Bob Jones Sr., independent Baptist patriarch, spoke often of his "colored friends," although in "everyday speech Jones slipped easily into common stereotypes."[63] But southern sectarian leaders argued with conviction that they had always been willing to help blacks, and that they had accomplished more than liberal reformers. "I've preached to, taught Bible classes for, and personally helped more Negroes than most of these do-gooders ever said 'Good Morning' to," wrote a Churches of Christ minister from Dora, Alabama, "but because we respect the customs of the ages and are not in favor of forced integration of the races, we are accused of being 'racists!' "[64] In a similar vein

61. *Southern Churches in Crisis,* p. 173. See also, Dollard, *Caste and Class,* pp. 385–386.

62. "Landslide in Texas Election for Dwight D. Eisenhower," *The Fundamentalist,* XXIX (August 1, 1952) , 2.

63. "Bob Jones: He Bridged the Gap," *Christianity Today,* XII (February 2, 1968) , 466.

64. Pryde E. Hinton, "The Sin of Mass Hatred," *Gospel Guardian,* XVIII (July 14, 1966) , 9.

conservative Baptist editor Noel Smith announced that he had "eaten with Negroes" when black nurses were "still changing the diapers of some of these little theological panty-waist revolutionaries."[65]

Southern sectarian leaders refused to listen to charges that southern whites had abused the blacks of the section. Bill Rice, Middle Tennessee conservative Baptist minister, admitted that the "white population" of his town had sometimes used the term "nigger" in the past but added that if the "Negro population" had ever been mistreated "I never was aware of it."[66] In fact, argued the dean of a conservative Baptist theological seminary, southern Negroes had prospered under the benevolent leadership of southern whites: "The truth of the matter is that colored people have the highest standard of living of any other place in the world—unless it be South Africa."[67] In 1961, Baptist editor Noel Smith curtly summed up the southern case: "The only genuine friend the Negro ever has had, has today, or ever will have are the white Anglo-Saxon Baptist's [sic] and Protestants."[68]

Black inequality, argued the conservatives, was rooted in black depravity.[69] "You can't legislate

65. "The 'Insight' King Brought McCall," *Baptist Bible Tribune,* XI (May 26, 1961) , 5.

66. "Dr. Bill Says," *Sword of the Lord,* XXXIV (September 6, 1968) , 1.

67. B. F. Dearmore, "The End of Civilization in Sight," *Orthodox Baptist,* XXXVII (August 1967) , 1.

68. "Straight for His Throat," *Baptist Bible Tribune,* XI (February 24, 1961) , 4.

69. For a general discussion of this argument, see Dollard, *Caste and Class,* pp. 367ff.

equality," urged a writer in a monthly published by
the Church of God of the Mountain Assembly, "people
have to deserve it and earn it."[70] Black profligacy was
considered by southern sectarians both a symbol of
Negro inferiority and a cause of it. Environment did
little to explain the degeneracy of southern blacks.
"The facts show," wrote a southern minister, "that it's
not the SLUMS which produce bums (these criminals
who call each other 'niggers') but bums produce the
slums."[71] In the wake of the Watts riot, the editor of the
national weekly of the Assemblies of God noted that
most of the rioters had been "liquor inflamed" and
reminded his readers, "It is significant that 'rioting
and drunkeness' are linked together in the Scriptures."
"What is needed in Watts," he concluded, "is an
evangelical church with white leadership."[72] In 1968,
Baptist editor John R. Rice called for a stop to the
"silly talk" about mistreatment of "minority groups
and ghetto poor." The problem was not environment,
cautioned Rice: "The simple truth is that poverty and
ignorance are a result of the wickedness of the human
heart. . . . Passing a law will not make somebody a
first-class citizen who has no character, no responsibility, who doesn't want to work."[73]

To many southern sectarians, black dissoluteness

70. "We Can't Legislate Happiness," *Gospel Herald,* XXVI (October 1966) , 10.
71. *Brother Mac's Weekly Report,* no volume (November 3, 1969) , 2.
72. [Robert C. Cunningham], "Watts—A Year Later," *Pentecostal
Evangel,* No. 2723 (July 17, 1966) , 4.
73. "Poor Can Be Good," *Sword of the Lord,* XXXIV (July 12,
1968) , 8.

made integration a vicious and immoral demand. One conservative Baptist preacher pointed out that in 1963 in Washington, D.C., 4,145 of the 4,529 cases of illegitimate births recorded were Negro babies.[74] Another Baptist minister announced that while he did not believe that blacks were inherently inferior, he was nonetheless concerned because "venereal disease was ten times as frequent among Negroes" and because "there are 16 times as many Negro dope addicts as white dope addicts."[75] Such statistical evidence led easily to highly charged emotional tirades. A Florida conservative asked, "Can you imagine yourself as a father of an attractive, intelligent, very dedicated 15 year old girl, forcing her to attend classes with 71 Negroes and only 18 white students?"[76] An independent Baptist minister bitterly protested the immorality of integration:

Do you think it is a *"Moral"* question when the Supreme Court . . . insists that little white girls attend the same school and use the same commode seats as Negroes with *ELEVEN times as many* VD, crab lice and germs? . . . Don't you pity a pure little girl, whose father would use such crooked reasoning & *allow her pure body be blighted by VD?*[77]

74. Hugh F. Pyle, "The Great Society," *Sword of the Lord,* XXXII (September 16, 1966), 8.

75. Rice, *Negro and White,* pp. 20–21.

76. *Brother Mac's Weekly Report,* no volume (January 19, 1970), 2.

77. James F. Dew, "Is He Hypocritical When Editor E. S. James Preaches Integration and Practices Segregation?" *Flag of Truth,* VI (September 1963), 20. See also, "Segregation Creating Serious Problems," *Brother Mac's Weekly Report,* no volume (June 30, 1969), 7; "Is This America?" *Orthodox Baptist,* XXXIX (January 1969), 3.

Such strong feeling was frequently rooted in a lingering Biblical scheme of white racism. Bob Jones Sr.
wrote a widely circulated pamphlet defending segregation as a "scriptural" racial arrangement.[78] In 1969,
a convention with some 200 delegates from conservative Baptist churches in Florida passed the following
resolution: "Both Hebrew and Christian civilizations
of the past and every denomination of Christianity
during the last 1900 years prior to this century have
held to the concept that segregation of the races in
social, religious and marital life is of divine command."[79] Southern preachers still pointed to the "curse
of Ham" to demonstrate the scriptural basis of Negro
inferiority.[80] In a book published in 1950, Paul F.
Beacham, president of Holmes Theological Seminary
and the most authoritative theological voice in the
Pentecostal Holiness church, was asked the question:
"Where did the negro [sic] come from?" Beacham
answered: "I believe the most reasonable theory is,
that the colored man came from Ham. . . . His descendants were as a consequence of the curse pro-
nounced upon him because of his irreverence, to be an

78. "Bob Jones: He Bridged the Gap," *Christianity Today*, XII
(February 2, 1968) , 466.

79. "Florida Southern Baptists Condemn Mongrelization," *Brother
Mac's Weekly Report*, no volume (September 29, 1969) , 2. It should
be said that some of the racially conservative sectarian preachers re-
jected such Biblical theories of black inferiority. See Rice, *Negro and
White*, pp. 5–7.

80. For a summary of these Biblical arguments, see Dollard, *Caste
and Class*, pp. 368–369; and Campbell and Pettigrew, *Christians in
Racial Crisis*, pp. 38–39, 50–53.

Southern sectarian leaders repeatedly warned that "race mixing" violated God's laws and would lead to a catastrophic "mongrelization" of the white race. In 1966, Sam E. Officer, leader of the Jesus church of Cleveland, Tennessee, sounded a typical alert: "From the beginning God created each race as it pleased Him and he has instructed that each race stay a pure race. . . . The birds have been more obedient than man."[88] A Primitive Baptist journalist also pointed out the conformity of the animal kingdom to God's laws: "The fact was brought out in Zoo Parade on T.V. that the lions are very much segregation minded, even with their own kind. . . . I believe that most of creation respects the laws of nature, except man."[89] Frequently those most concerned about the racial purity of whites denied that they believed Negroes were inferior. J. Royce Thomason, an independent pentecostal evangelist from Frederick, Oklahoma, assured his readers that he believed blacks "have souls that are just as precious as mine," but insisted that there were "certain differences in races" which "we must maintain."[90]

The sectarian protest against interracial marriages sometimes reached hysterical porportions. A rabid Texas Baptist preacher placed the following caption under a picture of Lyndon Johnson and a Negro

88. "The Ethopian Woman," *Light of the World,* XII (July, August, and September 1966), 7.

89. Muriel E. Johnson, "Whom Do We Fear, God or Man?" *Banner-Herald,* LXII (November 1956), 18.

90. "What Happened in Selma?" *Voice in the Wilderness,* no volume (July 1965), 8. See also, Bill Rice, "Dr. Bill Says," *Sword of the Lord,* XXXIV (November 29, 1968), 3; "News," *Bridegroom's Messenger,* LII (March 1964), 2.

White House secretary: "Civil Rights Lead to Mixed
Marriage. Want Your Girl to Have a Black Baby?"[91]
But perhaps the best example of sectarian anxiety is
the following poem published in 1961 in the official
organ of the International Apostolic and Missionary
Association, Incorporated, of Lakeland, Florida:

> When a white girl marries a negro, [*sic*]   2
> Her sun of life goes down,
> And glaring spots of sin appear on her
> White wedding gown.
>
> . . . .
> And white and black men stand aghast,
> While viewing this strange role:
> And mutter, "they will wreck themselves,
> And damn each other's souls."
>
> . . . .
> Three days and nights she felt black lips
> Press smug against her own.
> And on the fourth, her troubled soul,
> Let out a frightful groan.
> And so the weeks and months flew by,
> And then a baby came:
> She looked at it with tear-stained eyes,
> And hung her head with shame.
>
> . . . .
> I sold my birthright for a mess,
> I mixed my white-born blood
> With black blood, so I languish here like
> One bogged down in mud.
>
> . . . .

91. "Johnson's Negro Secretary," *Flag of Truth*, VII (October
1964), 1.

All other crimes may be forgiven when prayer
    its power fulfills;
The scheming crook may find new hope, and even
    the man that kills,
But all my prayers can never clear my baby's
    mongrel skin,
Nor make him white as driven snow, nor cleanse
    my soul of sin.
. . . .
Now, should I decide to leave him, where could
    I choose to go?
My mis-spent life will follow me like footprints
    in the snow.
Before me lie dark jungles where paramours seek
    a prey;
Behind me death keeps whispering, "I am the only
    way."

This black and white, prenuptial mess, this racial
    suicide;
Must be forbidden by the law, men must find racial
    pride!
Then, never again, forever, shall tales like mine
    unfold,
With all its shame, the saddest tale, that ever
    yet was told.[92]

Hysterical racism has probably declined slightly
among the sects since World War II, although examples of extremism are still not difficult to find, but
opposition to the civil rights movement by southern

92. Oliver Allstorm, "The Saddest Story Ever Told," *Apostolic
Evangel*, XXIV (January 1961) , 12–13.

church leaders has kept pace with the growth of reform movement. The urban riots and violence of the 1960s have repeatedly been the subjects of sensational stories in southern sectarian publications.[93] By 1965, even moderate civil rights leaders had become targets of vituperation in the religious press. A Virginia Churches of Christ leader charged that James J. Reeb, Boston minister who was killed in the Selma demon- strations of 1965, was not a "martyred saint" but rather a "murdered sinner."[94] Martin Luther King Jr. became symbolic of the religious agitator many southerners so deeply resented. The abuse heaped on King was awe- some. In a sermon following King's assassination, an independent Baptist minister made a typical attack: "Dr. Martin Luther King is no martyr to a peaceful cause, but rather a victim of his own hypocritical program of 'non-violence.' His funeral was a big farce! . . . It was a disgrace to our nation, our civil officials, and to real Christianity."[95]

A substantial portion of the sectarian press, and especially the politically-oriented independent Baptists journals, viewed the civil rights movement of the 1960s, and particularly the violence of the last half of the decade, as a part of an international Communist

93. See, for example, Wyatt Sawyer, "Sit-Ins, Riots and Demonstra- tions," *Firm Foundation*, LXXXII (September 28, 1965) , 616; E. Odell Thornton, "The Vicious Circle," *Herald of Truth*, XXII (July 1966) , 11; "The Radicals and Riots," *Voice of Freedom*, XVI (May 1968) , 73; M. L. Moser Jr., "Religious World Round-Up," *Baptist Challenge*, IX (March 1969) , 3, 9.

94. "Selma," *Christianity Today*, IX (April 23, 1965) , 797.

95. J. Cullis Smith, "The Sin of Violence or the Violent Death of Martin Luther King Jr.," *Orthodox Baptist*, XXXVIII (May 1968) , 2.

conspiracy. At best, civil rights leaders were classed as "ignorant do-gooders" who had fallen into "the Communist trap."[96] Religious liberals particularly seemed "dupes" to conservative churchmen. "I've never known an integrationist who was a good, sound Bible student," announced one sectarian preacher.[97] But charges against the civil rights movement were generally more pointed. In 1967, George S. Benson, nationally known rightwing conservative and Churches of Christ college president, warned the readers of the *Voice of Freedom* that "race agitation," particularly "in Northern U.S. cities," was a part of a Communist plot to win "America, the great Communist prize."[98] Particularly galling to conservatives was the liberal stance of the National Council of Churches of Christ; an article which purportedly paralleled the "objectives" of the liberal religious organization with those of the Communist party was repeatedly reprinted in southern sectarian journals.[99]

Civil rights activity was repeatedly linked directly to Communist conspiracy. Racial unrest was caused, wrote a leading independent Baptist evangelist, by "the

96. Richard P. Carter, "How Long?" *Voice of Revival,* I (August 1963) , 1. See also, Byon A. Jones, "From the Parson," *Reach,* XXXI (April 1965) , 14.

97. Campbell and Pettigrew, *Christians in Racial Crisis,* p. 50. Primitive Baptist editor J. Walter Hendricks wrote, "What these men [racial liberals] know about being a Christian, I could write in the palm of my hand." "Some Thoughts on Segregation," *Banner-Herald,* LXIII (May 1956) , 6.

98. "Negro Now Heads Communist Party," *Voice of Freedom,* XV (January 1967) , 15.

99. See, for instance, "Objectives of the Communist Party," *Baptist Banner,* II (January 1968) , 3; Roy J. Hearn, "The National Council of Churches," *Voice of Freedom,* XVII (May 1969) , 70–71.

socialists, the communists, the professional and paid
Negro leaders, and politicians who hope to gain votes,
raise enmities, hurl epithets, threaten force, and incite
hate."[100] In 1968, a San Antonio, Texas, Baptist minister
labeled Dick Gregory a "traitor" and charged that a
"majority of the Supreme Court" was "definitely
slanted toward the Communists."[101] Martin Luther
King Jr. was repeatedly branded "a tool in the hands
of the communists."[102] While most of his critics hesi-
tated to call King a Communist, there was wide agree-
ment with Tom Anderson's estimate that King was
"carrying out the Communist program more effectively
than any *known* American Communist."[103] Another
writer in the *Sword of the Lord* charged that King was
"known to associate with Communists" and that he
retained as "his chief lieutenants sex perverts and
identified Communists."[104]

Religious conservatives who linked civil rights activity with Communist conspiracy found ready allies in
such political-religious spokesmen as Billy James
Hargis and his Christian Crusade movement. Hargis's
anti-Communist programs and seminars have been
conspicuously crowded with conservative southern religious speakers, especially preachers from the

100. Rice, *Negro and White,* p. 3.

101. I. W. Rogers, "Facts Baptists Should Know," *Baptist Challenge,*
VIII (March 1968) , 1.

102. Victor E. Sears, "I Will Not be Intimidated to Silence," *Orthodox Baptist,* XXXVIII (May 1968) , 4.

103. Tom Anderson, "Martin Luther King," *Sword of the Lord,*
XXXIV (June 28, 1968) , 1.

104. Charles Poling, "How a Republic Died," *Sword of the Lord,*
XXXII (July 29, 1966) , 5.

Churches of Christ and independent Baptists.[105] On the other hand, when an independent Baptist minister recently compiled a list of the leading "defenders of the faith and our liberties" from "God-hating modernists and pink-fringed, Bible despising liberal prosocialists," he included "Carl McIntire, Billy James Hargis, Dan Smoot, Dr. John R. Rice, and Bob Jones University."[106] If Hargis is not simply a southern sectarian spokesman, the links between his movement and conservative southern religion are obviously quite strong.

As his recent biographer has pointed out, Hargis has never been primarily interested in race as an issue and has generally refrained from making overt segregationist pronouncements.[107] But his crusade against "left-wing" organizations has consistently aligned him against civil rights activists and kept him in the company of avowed racists.[108] Furthermore, Hargis has occasionally openly linked civil rights agitation with Communist conspiracy. In 1958, his *Christian Crusade* magazine contained a forboding warning:

Many Americans make a serious mistake in thinking of our racial troubles merely as a normal conflict between the

105. See, for instance, L. E. White Jr., "Robert Welch, Dr. Bob Jones Sr., Tom Anderson, Dr. G. Archer Weniger to Address Third Annual National Convention," *Christian Crusade*, XIII (June 1961), 3.

106. Hugh F. Pyle, "The Great Society," *Sword of the Lord*, XXXII (September 16, 1966), 8.

107. John Harold Redekop, *The American Far Right* (Grand Rapids, Michigan: W. B. Eerdmans Publishing Company, 1968), pp. 193–194.

108. *Ibid.*, pp. 39–40.

Negro and White races. . . . Behind the scenes a sinister force, the international communist conspiracy, has been stirring up this trouble for many years. As in all other drives of the Red Anti-Christ forces many innocent dupes have been taken in by the sugar-coating and do-good cloak surrounding this trouble-making agitation.[109]

More recently Hargis has written at great length about the communist's "satanic scheme to use American Negroes," and has boldly asserted that the National Association for the Advancement of Colored People and other civil rights organizations have historically had many "communist affiliations."[110]

A. B. McReynolds, another Oklahoma evangelist and radio preacher with a strong political orientation, has been much more outspoken on the race issue. McReynolds, whose influence in the South rivals that of Hargis, considered segregation a major plank in his anti-Communist campaign. He openly charged that Martin Luther King Jr. was a Communist and that his assassination was a part of an international conspiracy.[111] In 1968, when a northern civil rights paper labeled McReynolds's weekly paper a "Sh__rag,"[112] the incensed minister demanded that the "rotten chicken

109. Julian Williams, "Background of Our Racial Problem," *Christian Crusade,* X (March 1958) , 11.

110. Billy James Hargis, *The Far Left* (Tulsa: Christian Crusade, 1964) , pp. 261, 267–268; see pp. 259–268.

111. "Brother Mac Says," *Kiamichi Mission News,* XXVIII (July 1969) , 1.

112. "There Are Many Decent Negroes," *Brother Mac's Weekly Report,* no volume (October 14, 1968) , 2.

politicians" of the nation do something to protect the
rights of whites from black abuse.[113]

But if such independent evangelists were the most
widely known purveyors of conspiratorial schemes,
they had scores of lesser imitators on the South. A
Florida minister warned that integration was a double
conspiracy: "These race-mixers are ignorant of the
fact that their course will destroy both races and ruin
America; or they are willing tools for Zionism and
Communism to be used to destroy the white race and
take over America."[114] But most typical were the warnings of J. Royce Thomason, an Oklahoma pentecostal
evangelist. When the Civil Rights Act of 1965 was
being debated, Thomason published an ominous prediction about what passage would mean:

There will be an establishment of Federal reservations in
the predominately black states, governed by power crazed
bureaucrats. . . . This is almost an exact copy of a plan
that the Communists have had for years to establish a
Negro Communist Soviet in the South that will cover an
area of about 120,000 square miles and will mean that about
10 million whites will be driven from their homes. This
plan was discussed by Joseph Stalin in an address at Lenin
University where 2,000 American Communists were being
trained to take over America for the Communists. I will
send you a copy of a map that shows what areas the Com-

113. "Who Wrote This?" *Brother Mac's Weekly Report,* no volume
(November 3, 1969) , 1.
114. "Con't From Last Month," *Apostolic Evangel,* XXIV (January
1961) , 15.

munists plan to make into negro [*sic*] states if you will
write and ask for it.[115]

The turbulent racial conditions of the 1960s were a
rich source of inspiration for the cult-type prophets of
the South. Generally pessimistic in their view of the
world, such prophets usually considered racial conflict
another "sign" of the degenerate and hopeless condition. C. Parker Thomas, editor of the *Midnight Cry
Messenger* published in Southern Pines, North
Carolina, alerted his readers: "Actually the United
Nations, the Communists, the NAACP and other
agencies behind the integration movement are merely
pawns of Satan in his last great campaign to subdue the
earth." Thomas believed that integration was "of Satan
and actually started in the Garden of Eden"; those who
advocated the policy in the United States were "the
godless forces of anti-Christ." In fact, cautioned the
pentecostal evangelist, "joining hands with this anti-
Christ movement may be taking the 'mark of the
beast.' "[116] While there was some novelty in Thomas's
analysis of the spiritual causes of civil rights conflict,
his views were typical of a sizable group of radical
evangelists. They viewed race problems as an inevitable
consequence of the sinfulness of man and believed

115. "On the National and World Scene," *Voice in the Wilderness,*
no volume (June 1965), 6. See also, C. M. White, "Wanted: A Savior—
For America," *Pisgah,* XLII (June 1956), 1, 8; Hargis, *The Far Left,*
p. 262.
116. "The Real Power Behind Integration," *Midnight Cry Messenger,* VIII (May–June 1964), 3.

that such conflict would cease only with the impending return of Christ.[117]

Perhaps the most colorful of the prophets was R. G. Hardy, free-lance pentecostal faith healer with headquarters in Washington, D.C. Hardy published a monthly paper which was filled largely with rambling and voluminous revelations he received from the Lord; he sent the paper to those who supported his movement. Hardy's revelations frequently pointed to racial violence as God's punishment for the wickedness of the nation. In June 1967, Hardy revealed a prophecy for Washington, D.C.:

For behold, I would come down and speak to these my children that I might roll back again the curtain and let thine eyes behold what lies just before thee. For behold, saith the Lord, thou art on the threshold of dangerous and terrible days, saith the Lord God. A great destruction is determined for this city for the enemy has marked it, saith the Lord, that he might stir up unrest and set . . . race against race saith the Lord. . . . Yea, for this will be a bloody and a violent summer, saith the Lord.[118]

Hardy, and most other cult-type prophets, was pessimistic about solving racial discontent in the nation; he believed that only the vengeance of God would ultimately right whatever injustice existed. He wrote, "You can go to the cities all across America; There is

117. For some other examples, see "The March of Prophecy," *Voice of Healing*, XVII (September 1964) , 12; Juanita Coe, "Now Is the Time for Christians to Demonstrate!" *Christian Challenge*, XVII (October 1967) , 2–3.

118. "Thus Saith the Lord!" *Faith in Action*, VI (June 1967) , 5.

[*sic*] no churches, no preachers, no spirit: The night
has come. It's hard to get on radio stations anymore;
The night is coming. The mystery of inquity doth
already work."[119] A "Jesus only" pentecostal evangelist
reflected the same prophetic pessimism about the in-
ability of religious reform to solve social violence:

As violence rises, the savor of the salt decreases. The church
. . . is laughed at. The once snarling tiger who fought and
slashed at sin, crime, and liquor from the pulpit, is now a
mere tame house cat. . . . Her blood pressure is low, her
energy dissipated and her once healthful color has faded
into a wan pale shade of unconcern. And amidst it all, the
coming of the Lord nears!!![120]

But if racial violence led to prophetic despair in a
radical portion of the southern sectarian community, it
spured others into energetic activity. Some church
leaders called for renewed zeal in programs to evange-
lize blacks. B. C. Goodpasture, leading editor in the
Churches of Christ, sounded the alarm in 1946:

The colored people of this country need the gospel. . . .
If the gospel is not preached to them in its purity, they
will fall into the meshes of some of the present-day "isms."
Both the Catholic and the Communist look upon the
colored man as a promising prospect.[121]

Most of the larger white sects in the South agreed that
religion should play a more active role in controlling

119. "The Rise of the Anti-Christ," *Faith in Action,* VI (October
1967) , 2.
120. A. D. VanHoose, "Signs of the Times," *Herald of Truth,* XXIV
(June 1968) , 4.
121. "Help Brother Cassius," *Gospel Advocate,* LXXXVIII (December 5, 1946) , 1140.

black radicalism. The remedy for black violence was black Christians.[122] Indeed, it was this sense of urgency which gave financial stability to many of the independent evangelists of the South. As early as 1958, Billy James Hargis used "racial unrest" to sell his services:

If God's people, irregardless of political preferences or denominational affiliations, do not rise up and finance an anti-communist Crusade such as Christian Crusade with their possessions and time, 1959 may well be the year that freedom is completely killed and communism triumphs.[123]

In 1968, an Atlanta Assemblies of God minister urged financial support for "qualified Negro ministers" throughout the South. Blacks had lost confidence in white Christians and only by supporting black ministers could Negroes be provided "the spiritual leadership they so desperately need in this crisis hours."[124]

In addition to mission work among the blacks, southern sectarian leaders advocated a program of patriotism and respect for the law. By the 1960s, law and order had become a fetish in the southern sectarian press. The civil rights movement had become synonymous with lawlessness. "Since the federal Brown decision in 1954," wrote an independent Baptist minister, "the law has abandoned its impartial majesty

122. See "Passing and Permanent," *Pentecostal Evangel,* No. 1898 (September 23, 1950) , 7.
123. "Racial Troubles in America," *Christian Crusade,* X (December 1958) , 9.
124. L. Calvin Bacon, "Eyewitness at a Funeral," *Pentecostal Evangel,* No. 2827 (July 14, 1968) , 21.

and become a tool of favoritism and social distortion."[125]
Another independent Baptist, alarmed by black rioting
in 1968, warned, "America has gone far down the road
to socialism, godlessness, and it has been helped on
that road by an atheistic Supreme Court, liberals
turned out of modern, godless universities and by the
soft-hearted do-gooders who never learned the funda-
mentals of good citizenship."[126] A Cumberland Presbyterian, disgruntled by the liberal racial pronouncements of some of her church's leaders, expressed a
widely held sectarian sentiment in 1968: "The whole
nation is in urgent need of sermons and articles on
'Law and Order.' "[127]

The defense of law and order came naturally out of
a strong patriotic strain in the thought of most southern
sects. Whatever the race problems of this country,
suggested a minister of the Pentecostal Church of God
of America, "the United States still offers more oppor-
tunity and personal freedom than practically any other

125. Thurman Sensing, "A Call to Law and Order," *Sword of the
Lord,* XXXIV (September 27, 1968), 11.

126. "Justice Abe Fortas for Lawbreaking," *Sword of the Lord,*
XXXIV (October 11, 1968), 12.

127. Elizabeth White Sevier, "Ministers, Listen to Laymen," *Cumberland Presbyterian,* CXL (June 11, 1968), 11. For some other exam-
ples, see LeRoy Johnson, "Civil Disobedience," *Pentecostal Evangel,*
No. 2827 (July 14, 1968), 8; John McDowell, "How Sick Society Is
Destroying Religion," *Emmanuel Holiness Messenger,* III (April 1969),
2–3; Arnie M. Cribb, "Today's Need—Christian Citizens," *Pentecostal
Holiness Advocate,* XLVIII (March 20, 1965), 4–5; "The March of
Prophecy," *Voice of Healing,* XIX (April 1966), 12; Kenneth Wood-
ward, "Demonstrators and the New Morality," *World Revival,* XII
(November–December 1968), 14–15; Bill Millwood, "Law Must Pre-
vail," *Cumberland Presbyterian,* CXL (June 18, 1968), 11.

country in the world."[128] The patriotic stance of a
large segment of southern sectarianism was well stated
in a resolution passed in 1966 by the National Association of Evangelicals: "We challenge all loyal
Americans to let their appreciation of the U.S.A. be
known by every legitimate means. For too long loyal
Americans have sat back and watched with dismay the
erosion and disintegration of many of our divinely-
bestowed freedoms."[129]

In sum, sectarian literature since 1945 is a mirror of
southern racist thought. In the sects can be found
spokesmen for virtually every conservative racial idea,
from moderate segregationists to demented hate-
mongers. Each argument, many of them as old as race
relations in the South, is buttressed by fervent consciences, Biblical prooftexts, and the holy blessing of
an anointed spokesman for God. The collective views
may tell little about the mind of God; they tell much
about the mind of white southerners.

128. George L. Ford, "Is Patriotism Sinful?" *Pentecostal Messenger*,
XXXVI (July 1962), 3.
129. "I Pledge Allegiance," *Pentecostal Holiness Advocate*, L (June
25, 1966), 2. See also, "A Tired American Speaks Out," *Pentecostal
Free Will Baptist Messenger*, XIX (September 1, 1966), 2; John D.
Overcash, "Government," *Gospel Messenger*, XXXV (January 1,
1960), 5.

Chapter 4

INTEGRATION AND THE SECTS

T HE identification of sectarian religion with con- servative political and social views has been ab- solute in the minds of most Americans. Scholars have persistently stereotyped "the social ideas of fundamen- talism" as "quite traditional."[1] William G. McLough- lin's assessment of the social and political thrust of sectarian religion is extreme: "The new evangelicals are the spiritual hard-core of the radical right,"[2] even though the vocal racism of many southern religious conservatives lends credibility to such judgments.

But southern sectarian leaders have increasingly protested such characterizations. The editor of *Christi- anity Today* was obviously piqued by McLoughlin's charge:

Now it must be admitted that there is some truth in this description. . . . Nevertheless, it is not a political philos- ophy or an economic commitment that binds the evangeli- cals together. Evangelicals do not exclude either Democrats

1. Daniel Bell, ed., *The Radical Right* (Garden City, New York: Doubleday, 1963), p. 21; see pp. 19–21, 50–52. See also, Richard Hofstadter, *Anti-Intellectualism in American Life* (New York: Knopf, 1963), pp. 133–136.
2. William G. McLoughlin and Robert N. Bellah, eds., *Religion in America* (Boston: Houghton Mifflin, 1968), p. 63.

or Republicans, nor are they prone to exalt their social and economic views to creedal stature. . . . They are also found in every walk of life. They are politicians, laborers, bankers, social workers, performing artists, writers, ministers, and civil servants.[3]

The reaction to McLoughlin's article was unquestionably strong; when it was reprinted the author admitted that he had "received several thoughtful letters which tax me with being too dogmatic in asserting the ultraconservatism of all Evangelicals." He confided that he had been "led to modify my position."[4] Southern sectarianism is simply not all of a piece. Moderate and liberal racial views emanated from some unexpected sources in the post–World War II years.

One stream of liberal racial thought in southern sectarianism has its source in the growing sophistication of many of the sects since World War II. The latent denominational character of the older southern churches—Baptist, Methodist and Presbyterian—has been an obvious fountainhead of moderate racial expressions.[5] The same transition toward denominationalism has taken place in the older and more prosperous sects of the section. The young people reared in the southern sects in the 1950s and 1960s flooded into the liberal arts colleges and graduate schools of North and South. A coterie of educated, middle-class members

3. "Who Are the Evangelicals?" *Christianity Today*, XI (June 23, 1967), 958–959.

4. McLoughlin and Bellah, *Religion in America*, pp. 71–72.

5. See Kenneth K. Bailey, *Southern White Protestantism* (New York: Harper and Row, 1964), pp. 130–158; Dwight W. Culver, *Negro Segregation in the Methodist Church* (New Haven: Yale University Press, 1953), pp. 148–170.

has brought to many of the sects a new measure of social concern and racial liberalism. In 1964, the National Association of Evangelicals passed a resolution calling on "all men to support on all levels of government such ordinances and legislation as will assure all people those freedoms guaranteed in our Constitution." The leaders of the association pointed with "thanksgiving" to an integrated Easter service recently conducted by Billy Graham in Birmingham, Alabama.[6]

The emergence of sect leaders with moderate racial views was perhaps most impressive in the Churches of Christ. A number of forces pushed the group toward a more moderate position by the 1960s. Northern church members repeatedly denounced the image of the group as a "sectional church," and one northerner warned in 1963, "The churches of Christ in the South will have to make up their minds whether they are going to serve God or still hallow God and serve customs and traditions of men as they have in the past."[7] The minister of a church in New London, Connecticut, reminded the southern churches that "in this day and time" the "practice of an individual church is not only her own concern, but it also reflects a certain image for the brotherhood." Segregation in southern churches, he argued, could only result in the Churches of Christ being "labeled a racist sect."[8]

6. "N. A. E. and Civil Rights," *Christianity Today,* VIII (May 8, 1964) , 50.

7. B. R. Loy, "U.S. Is Under World Wide Indictment," *Christian Chronicle,* XXI (December 13, 1963) , 2.

8. Roy Bowen Ward, "Fundamental Issue at Stake Is Teaching on Church Unity," *Christian Chronicle,* XXI (October 18, 1963) , 4.

But moderate concern in the Churches of Christ was not limited to northerners who feared the group would be branded a "racist sect." The colleges of the church, while hardly bastions of liberalism, unquestionably exerted a mellowing influence. In 1963, a young minister wrote, "As a Son of the South, I once ardently defended segregation. . . . While a student at Abilene Christian College, I learned the way of the Lord more accurately."[9] By the mid-1960s, a number of influential church leaders had begun to speak out against racial injustice. John Allen Chalk, speaker on the "Herald of Truth" national radio broadcast, preached a series of messages in 1968 dealing "in part with the evil of racial prejudice and hatred."[10] A number of publications within the group reflected the liberal mood; perhaps the most important of the new socially conscious journals was *Mission,* published in Abilene, Texas, with an influential board of editors.[11]

Probably the most significant symptom of the growing social awareness in the Churches of Christ has been the controversial editorial course followed by one of the older church periodicals, the *Christian Chronicle.* The policy of the paper has been provocative throughout the decade; at times the journal has openly espoused liberal social views and flirted with theological liberalism. Of course, the stand of the *Christian*

9. *Ibid.*

10. Dudley Lynch, "Coverage, Comments Mark Vigor of Racial Debate," *Christian Chronicle,* XXV (November 4, 1968), 4.

11. For an example of the social approach of *Mission,* see Hubert G. Locke, "Discipleship in the Inner City," *Mission,* I (August 1967), 19–20.

Chronicle has been bold only in the context of the Churches of Christ, but within that context, the editors have been branded "pink as pink can be" and accused of trying "to destroy the church we love."[12] The heat engendered by the weekly has led to a series of editorial changes in the past decade, but the central message of social activism and moderation has remained unchanged.

James W. Nichols, editor of the *Christian Chronicle* in 1963, opened the flood gates in the Churches of Christ when he publicly solicited the views of his readers on racial problems. He captured well the attitude of the older leaders of the church about public discussion of the issue: "Have you noticed the silence of our gospel papers on this topic? Have you noticed how our preachers can somehow preach everything under the sun except this ticklish situation?"[13] Nichols was no crusader; when flooded with answers to his appeal, he quickly disavowed any intention to "stir up some kind of church fuss."[14] But the gates had been opened and they were never again completely closed in the Churches of Christ. Condemnations of "detached neutrality" and demands that church leaders stop "pussyfooting about human relations" became a permanent part of the intellectual baggage of the Churches of Christ.[15]

12. James W. Nichols, "A Restatement of Editorial Policy," *Christian Chronicle*, XXIII (August 19, 1966), 2.

13. "Let's Discuss the Negro Issue," *Christian Chronicle*, XX (September 27, 1963), 2.

14. "Not a 'Brotherhood' Issue," *Christian Chronicle*, XXI (October 25, 1963), 2.

15. L. Denton Crews Jr., "Church Has Remained Quiet Too Long on Negro Problem," *Christian Chronicle*, XXI (October 18, 1963), 4.

Nichols reported that he had received "several" letters opposing integration but that "most . . . were for it—and these came from North *and* South."[16] Of course, the editor's experience probably reflected as much about the limited circulation of the *Christian Chronicle* as it did about the racial views of a majority of the members of the Churches of Christ. Old prejudices remained strong, but by the mid-1960s, moderate racial views and interracial programs had an articulate group of supporters within the church. In the fall of 1968 an interracial "Conference on Race Relations" was held in Atlanta; fifty ministers discussed "improving race relations in the Churches of Christ."[17] A Texas conservative's reaction to the conference was stunned disbelief: "Are you sure they were of the church of Christ? . . . I pray these were not of the Lord's church."[18] But the resolve of the young liberals was clear. Jennings Davis, dean of students at Pepperdine College, penned a liberal ultimatum: "The Churches of Christ must end the image they have as a racially segregated group."[19]

The Cumberland Presbyterian church also contained a strong element of racial liberals by the 1960s.

16. "Not a 'Brotherhood' Issue," *Christian Chronicle*, XXI (October 25, 1963), 2.

17. "Conference on Race Relations," *Mission*, II (September 1968), 24–26. See also, " 'Cooling Breeze' Hits Chicago During Summer," *Christian Chronicle*, XXIII [*sic*, XXIV] (October 28, 1966), 3; Carroll Pitts Jr., "Politics and the Negro Revolution," *Mission*, I (June 1968), 7–12.

18. "Sown in Atlanta," *Christianity Today*, XIII (October 11, 1968), 16.

19. Dudley Lynch, "Coverage, Comments Mark Vigor of Racial Debate," *Christian Chronicle*, XXV (November 4, 1968), 1.

Something of a moderate tradition existed in the group throughout the postwar period. As early as 1948, editor Ky Curry of the *Cumberland Presbyterian,* who sometimes revealed marked racial prejudice, indicated that the church was soon going to have to look "purposefully and frankly at the racial question" out of "stark necessity."[20] After a major organizational realignment in the group in 1948, the leadership of the church was composed overwhelmingly of theological and social moderates. In 1954, Hugh Morrow, executive secretary of the Board of Missions and Evangelism and a graduate of the Vanderbilt Divinity School, chided the church for its "self-righteous complacency" on the race question and praised the Supreme Court's school integration decision.[21] C. Ray Dobbins, new editor of the *Cumberland Presbyterian,* also urged church members to "do all we can to prepare people to conform to this new ruling." Perhaps such good work would do something to hide the "shame" of the church's long silence.[22] This liberal activism among the leadership of the group led to the passage of a mild resolution supporting the court decision at the General Assembly of the church in 1955.[23]

Dobbins became something of a civil rights activist

20. "Heating the Old Branding Iron," *Cumberland Presbyterian,* CXIX (February 5, 1948) , 3.
21. "The Question of Segregation of Races," *Cumberland Presbyterian,* CXXVI (February 16, 1954) , 8–9.
22. "Let Me Say," *Cumberland Presbyterian,* CXXVI (June 8, 1954) , 5.
23. "Report on General Assembly," *Cumberland Presbyterian,* CXXVII (July 5, 1955) , 5.

in his role as editor of the church's weekly paper. In 1968, he termed race relations "the most urgent domestic issue in the country today" and called for an "increasing number of relations between black and white people on all levels of life and society."[24] Dobbins participated in the efforts to mediate the Memphis garbage strike in 1968[25] and was stunned and ashamed when Martin Luther King was assassinated in Memphis, "the theological and political center of my church."[26] In a sober editorial, he called for "a resurrection of a Christian conscience" to heal the wounds of the nation.[27]

As early as 1948, the Cumberland Presbyterian church showed a renewed interest in the Colored Cumberland Presbyterian church. The convention passed a resolution that year offering "assistance, cooperation, and financial aid" to the black group.[28] In the late 1950s, the church appointed an official "Committee on Cooperation and Union with the Colored C. P. Church." At the General Assembly of the church in 1960, the committee urged "fraternal exchanges" between the white and black churches, passed a "social creed" which was fairly liberal but then concluded:

24. "More Human and Humane Relations," *Cumberland Presbyterian*, CXL (February 13, 1968), 5.

25. C. Ray Dobbins, "Listening in Order to Create a Climate of Understanding," *Cumberland Presbyterian*, CXL (March 5, 1968), 5.

26. "What Can We Say to the Church," *Cumberland Presbyterian*, CXL (April 30, 1968), 5.

27. *Ibid.* See also, "What Church Leaders in Memphis Say to the Church," *Cumberland Presbyterian*, CXL (April 30, 1968), 8–9, 12, 14.

28. "C. P. Church Manifests Interest in Negro C. P. Church," *Cumberland Presbyterian*, CXX (July 1, 1948), 2.

"We feel that the time has hardly come when Cumberland Presbyterians can be reunited into one body."[29] Such union should remain a "necessary goal," but it could not be rushed to fruition.[30] Racial liberals did succeed in providing for the admission of black "ministerial students" to the church's seminary in 1953 and to Bethel College in 1961.[31] But the liberals of the late sixties were not satisfied with these minor achievements. In 1967, Hubert Morrow wrote, "I confess that local congregations are still segregated with respect to Negroes. . . . All these things I confess, together with my personal sins of timidity in the face of custom and prejudice."[32]

Racial liberals in the Cumberland Presbyterian church pushed hard in the late sixties to consummate a reunion with the Negro wing of the movement; they considered the step the "door to our own salvation from prejudice."[33] A Nashville minister wrote,

29. "Reports to Assembly," *Cumberland Presbyterian,* CXXXII (June 14, 1960), 14.

30. *Ibid.*

31. See L. B. Tenskey, "An Address at General Assembly," *Cumberland Presbyterian,* CXXVI (July 20, 1954), 7; "The Assembly at a Glance," *Cumberland Presbyterian,* CXXXII (July 5, 1960), 3. Opposition obviously remained strong. See "What's Your Opinion?" *Cumberland Presbyterian,* CXXVI (November 9, 1954), 7.

32. "Conditions of Our Fellowship," *Cumberland Presbyterian,* CXXXIX (July 4, 1967), 8–9. In the late 1960s the "Issues in the Church" column in the *Cumberland Presbyterian,* written by Roy E. Blakeburn, was a persistent source of liberal racial expression. See also, Thomas H. Campbell, *Good News on the Frontier* (Memphis: Frontier Press, 1965), p. 81.

33. Hubert Covington, "What the Second C. P. Church Has to Offer Us," *Cumberland Presbyterian,* CXL (February 13, 1968), 12.

Only as the Cumberland Presbyterian Church finds forgiveness for its prejudiced attitudes and discriminating practices can it be redeemed. The two churches being brought together in fellowship would hopefully offer us a greater challenge and desire to seek forgiveness. This could be God's voice calling us to repentance.[34]

But every overture to reunite proposed by the white church failed to win the approval of the Negro group.[35] Liberals have continued to press the issue, in spite of formidable resistance.[36]

The 1968 and 1969 General Assemblies of the Cumberland Presbyterian church clearly revealed the deep internal tensions within the group. At the 1968 convention the liberals were badly disappointed; one charged that the assembly was "vague, ambiguous and contradicted both itself and the church's historic position." The clash centered around the desire of "a large number of commissioners" to "see the church make a statement against lawlessness, riot, destruction and violence." This move, wrote one reporter, was a "racially motivated" effort to "see our Memphis leaders reprimanded." The resolution which was passed had precisely that effect; it condemned "civil disobedience" and announced that no church official

34. *Ibid.*

35. See "Second C. P. Church Holds 93rd Session," *Cumberland Presbyterian,* CXXXIX (July 11, 1967), 13; "Cumberland Presbyterian Church," *Christianity Today,* XI (July 21, 1967), 1058; 1960 *Minutes* General Assembly Cumberland Presbyterian Church (Memphis: Cumberland Presbyterian Church, 1960), pp. 190–200; and, generally, the July 1967, issues of the *Cumberland Presbyterian.*

36. See C. Ray Dobbins, "Yesterday's Answers to Today's Crises," *Cumberland Presbyterian,* CXL (February 20, 1968), 5.

involved in social reform should claim to "represent the denomination in any official capacity." A dejected liberal wrote, "As the foregoing indicates, Jonah swallowed the whale at the Assembly and little was done in a way of positive approach to social issues."[37]

The battle reopened at the 1969 convention. A liberal minister cast down the gauntlet: "We will speak to the issues."[38] In the highly charged sessions, liberals succeeded in passing a new resolution calling for union with the black wing of the movement, repealed the 1968 resolution on civil disobedience, and flooded the program with militant black speakers.[39] The cleavage in the church was deep, but by the end of the decade Cumberland Presbyterian leadership was overwhelmingly liberal.[40]

Liberal forces were not so strong in most southern sects, but few of the larger groups were without a moderate element on the race issue. In 1965, at its annual meeting in Raleigh, North Carolina, the National Association of Free Will Baptists passed a resolution encouraging its churches "to bring every person into a right relationship with God, regardless

37. Turner N. Clinard, "Social Issues," *Cumberland Presbyterian* CXL (July 9, 1968), 9, 11. See also, C. Ray Dobbins, "Facing Differences with Dialogue—Not Diatribe," *Cumberland Presbyterian,* CXL (August 6, 1968), 5.

38. Roy E. Blakeburn, "A Mood of Chastened Hope," *Cumberland Presbyterian,* CXLI (August 5, 1969), 11.

39. See *Ibid.;* Don L. Coleman, "The Church's Mission; How It Was Expressed at Assembly," *Cumberland Presbyterian,* CXLI (July 22, 1969), 8–9.

40. C. Ray Dobbins, "Facing Differences with Dialogue—Not Diatribe," *Cumberland Presbyterian,* CXL (August 6, 1968), 5.

of race or national origin." The assembly recognized "the right and privilege of the local church to conduct its own affairs in the area of human relations" but offered the judgment that "we must learn to be tolerant."[41]

The Church of God made some significant moves toward better race relations in the 1960s. Although few of the church's leaders were social activists, and their major concern was maintaining peace and solidarity within the group, the Church of God became in 1964 perhaps the first southern church to integrate completely its black members into the organization of the church.[42] In its national assembly at Dallas in the same year a "Resolution on Human Rights" was passed "without dissent" which urged that no American "be deprived of his right to worship, vote, rest, eat, sleep, be educated, live and work on the same basis as other citizens."[43] Church leaders usually avoided the question, but occasionally moderate views were expressed. In 1964, R. H. Gause, Dean of Lee Bible College in Cleveland, Tennessee, warned against the

41. "Free Will Baptists Take Racial Stand," *Christianity Today,* IX (August 27, 1965) , 1202.

42. See *Minutes* of the 50th General Assembly of the Church of God (Cleveland, Tennessee: Church of God Publishing House [1964]) , p. 28. David Reimers notes that "as of 1965 the Protestant Episcopal Church was the only major denomination with a sizable membership of both Negroes and southern whites that had achieved desegregation of its southern dioceses." *White Protestantism and the Negro* (New York: Oxford University Press, 1965) , p. 123; see pp. 158–161.

43. *Minutes* of the 50th General Assembly of the Church of God, pp. 67–68. See also, "Resolution on Human Rights," *Church of God Evangel,* LIV (September 14, 1964) , 15; "For Such a Time," *Christianity Today,* VIII (September 11, 1964) , 52.

use of religion to justify "social oppressions" such as "racial prejudice and strictly social discrimination." Such actions, he counseled, gave a ring of truth to the Marxist accusation that religion was the "opiate of the people."[44] By the end of the decade of the sixties, liberal leaders in the group were consciously trying to change the sectarian image of the Church of God.[45] At least a few of them recognized that a major contribution to that cause would be a "breakthrough to better human relations" based on the "guiding principle" that " 'God is no respecter of persons.' "[46] Few leaders of the Church of God were social radicals, but neither did they totally ignore the national racial crises of the 1960s.

Most of the major southern pentecostal sects included similar moderate elements. At the 1969 convention of the Assemblies of God in Dallas, an appeal for action in the "inner city" and the black ghettos was well received, although it brought no action.[47] Even the staunchly conservative Pentecostal Holiness church has shown some interest in race relations. At the 1965 General Conference of the church, the General Executive Board was instructed to "seek to establish communication with sincere religious leaders among

44. "Religion May Become an Opiate of the People," *Church of God Evangel,* LIV (September 21, 1964), 14.
45. "Evangelicals Concerned and Committed," *Church of God Evangel,* LIX (June 9, 1969), 10–11.
46. Jack Smith, "Social Action and the Church," *Church of God Evangel,* LVIII (January 27, 1969), 8.
47. "Assemblies of God: Fair Skies at Dallas," *Christianity Today,* XIII (September 26, 1969), 1149.

American Negroes; that an effort be made to form Negro Associate Conferences, and that in general sincere action be focused toward constructively assisting our Negro friends with the moral and spiritual problems which are so prevalent and so pressing."[48] Moderate racial pleas occasionally found their way into the publications of the church.[49] Vincent Synan, a recent Ph.D. graduate at the University of Georgia, a Pentecostal Holiness minister and the son of the chief executive of the church, argues that there is a growing liberal social spirit among the younger generation in the sect.[50] Synan's appraisal of the social relevance of pentecostalism may be overdrawn, but his concern about the racial image of the Pentecostal Holiness church is probably typical of many of the sect's young ministers. Of course, a majority of the church probably still agrees with the young historian's father: "People can be saved without becoming crusaders for segregation or integration."[51] But change is in the wind.

In the early 1950s, George A. Turner, editor of the "Sunday School Lesson" in the *Pentecostal Herald,* organ of the National Holiness Association published in Asbury, Kentucky, began including in his lessons such unexpected quips as "The Bible is at least as

48. Quoted in Harold Vinson Synan, "The Pentecostal Movement in the United States" (unpublished Ph.D. dissertation, University of Georgia, 1967), p. 135.
49. See, for instance, Byon A. Jones, "From the Parson," *Reach,* XXXI (April 1965), 15.
50. Synan, "The Pentecostal Movement."
51. J. A. Synan, "Meeting in Chicago," *Pentecostal Holiness Advocate,* XLVIII (May 9, 1964), 8.

emphatic in condemning race prejudice as in promoting 'second blessing holiness.' "[52] By the 1960s
Turner's attitude was reflected throughout the influential holiness magazine. "A major issue before the
American people, both majority and minority races,"
wrote Turner in 1965, "is whether or not love will
prevail or whether hatred and resentment will in-
crease. . . . Are minority groups welcome in your
church?"[53] Beginning in 1965, the National Holiness
Association passed a series of moderate civil rights
resolutions. Typical was a 1968 proposal condemning
"open and *de facto* discrimination" but at the same
time opposing "irresponsible and violent methods to
achieve human rights."[54]

Clearly, by the 1960s the rumblings of social concern
could be heard throughout the sectarian South. Many
of the "new evangelicals" proudly looked on this new
social conscience as a symptom of the growing maturity
and sophistication of their sects. In 1965, during racial
demonstrations in Alabama, *Christianity Today*
boasted that "evangelical involvement is believed to
have been without precedent in the current civil rights
movement."[55] Timothy Smith's influential book, *Revivalism and Social Reform in Mid-Nineteenth
Century America,* a study of social activism during the

52. *Pentecostal Herald,* LXII (August 22, 1951), 12.
53. "Sunday School Lesson," *Pentecostal Herald,* LXXIX (September 1, 1965), 16.
54. "NHA Report on Social Action," *Pentecostal Herald,* LXXIX
(July 31, 1968), 16.
55. "The March to Montgomery," *Christianity Today,* IX (April 9,
1965), 746.

early holiness movement, pricked the consciences of many middle-class conservatives. To many sectarian leaders the obvious message in Smith's book was that conservative religion and social reform were not irreconcilable themes.[56] After reading the book, one influential pentecostal editor urged his readers to seriously consider the impact of the idea that "revivalism and social reform . . . were actually father and son in mid-nineteenth century America."[57]

Of course, the growth of moderate racial feeling was probably less marked in the sects of the South than in the older denominations. Samuel S. Hill Jr. accounts for this new social liberalism in the traditional churches of the South by the emergence of a new "upper class, the cosmopolitan citizens in the new society."[58] The social views of southern sects have also keenly reflected the urbanization of the South and the affluence of postwar America.

Professor Hill suggests that this social liberalism among the upper-class segment of the South is a departure from traditional behavior in the section: "Historically, in the South and in the nation generally, protests have come from the disinherited, the down and out, the economically and psychically deprived."[59] In fact, both types of social protest have always been and

56. See Timothy L. Smith (New York and Nashville: Abingdon Press, 1957) ; "Evangelicals and Public Affairs," *Christianity Today,* XIII (January 17, 1964) , 24.

57. "Pentecost and Politics," *Pentecost,* No. 47 (March 1959) , 17.

58. *Southern Churches in Crisis* (New York: Holt, Rinehart and Winston, 1967) , pp. 182–183.

59. *Ibid.,* p. 182; see pp. 182–189.

remain present in the South. In the last century and a half the Methodist and Baptist churches in the South have changed from lower-class sects into middle-class and upper-class denominations. But it would be a mistake to assume that there were no middle- and upper-class churches in the South during the nineteenth century; it is equally obvious that lower-class sects still exist in the South. Is it true that such radical religious groups no longer "protest" the social injustices in their society?

The social views of the churches of the poor have generally been ignored by scholars. The more radical a sect, the less visible it is. Seriously deprived people, especially white people, probably form a proportionately smaller segment of the population of the nation than in the past. But the disinherited are still present, especially in the South, and their churches reflect the same social erraticism which has always characterized such groups. The boldest challenges to southern racial taboos have come not from middle-class denominationalism but from the more extreme forms of sect-and-cult religion in the South. It is only at this level in southern society that one can find open exceptions to David Reimers statement: "Apart from the few white churches that included Negroes, either as members or attenders, Protestants found few opportunities for interracial contact."[60]

The Church of God of Prophecy was probably the largest racially mixed church in the South from 1945

---

60. *White Protestantism and the Negro,* p. 161.

until the mid-1960s. Unlike the larger pentecostal sects, the Church of God of Prophecy never separated its black members into a satellite organization. While local churches have generally been either black or white, the state assemblies, international assemblies, and church institutions have been integrated throughout the history of the sect.[61] The church's "Bible Training Camps" have provided religious, social, and recreational opportunities for the young of the church to associate on an integrated basis.[62] Tomlinson College, located in Cleveland, Tennessee, began its operation in 1968 on an integrated basis.[63]

Leaders of the Church of God of Prophecy did not parade their flouting of the social customs of the South, but neither were they timorous. They unquestionably did not consider themselves social liberals; they were little interested in civil rights as a political issue. The sect was simply committed to religious racial equality. Ralph C. Scotten, black minister and church official, stated a fundamental assumption of the sect in 1948: "One of the chief aims of the Church was to gather

61. See "Here and There with Pictures During the Assembly," *White Wing Messenger,* XXII (September 28, 1946), 3–4; "Announcing Three Bible Training Camps for 1960!" *White Wing Messenger,* XXXVII (February 20, 1960), 9; "Building Purchased and Dedicated at Richmond, Virginia," *White Wing Messenger,* XLVI (April 26, 1969), 7. For a contradictory example, see "Camp Potomac," *Wings of Truth,* XXVIII (November 1966), 4.

62. See "Good News, Everybody," *White Wing Messenger,* XXVIII (February 17, 1951), 4.

63. "Seventeen Graduates from Tomlinson College," *White Wing Messenger,* XLVI (July 19, 1969), 5.

the children of God together in one church, under one government with Christ as the head."[64] An article in the *White Wing Messenger* in 1965 summed up the racial thought of the sect:

To have racial distinction would be against the will of God or the purpose of the Church. . . . The speckled bird has many different colored feathers, and so is the Church of the last days. . . . I feel like shouting when I think of the oneness that is to be found in Christ Jesus.[65]

It would be a mistake to label such views "liberal"; nonetheless, the Church of God of Prophecy was committed to a religious program of biracialism and a theology of racial equality rarely found in the larger sects of the South.

Many small southern sects demonstrated a willingness to tamper with the racial code of the section. The Church of God (Jerusalem Acres) located in Cleveland, Tennessee, is typical. The sect is composed of about twenty congregations;[66] some of the local churches are black and some white. But the general assemblies of the sect are totally integrated: one of its twelve Apostles is black, two of the sect's counselors are black, as is one of the seven General Overseers of Church Auxiliaries. Negro and white ministers work inter-

64. "All Races in One Mighty Church," *White Wing Messenger,* XXV (December 11, 1948), 1. See also, G. W. Bafford, "Wanted: Missionary to the Colored in Mississippi," *White Wing Messenger,* XXIV (January 4, 1947), 3.

65. E. A. Crossfield, "The Church Is Not Subject to Racial or National Frontiers," *White Wing Messenger,* XLII (June 5, 1965), 6.

66. Interview with Chief Bishop Marion W. Hall, Cleveland, Tennessee, August 14, 1969.

changeably with black and white congregations.[67] Chief Bishop Marion W. Hall, although opposed to intermarriage of the races, has been outspoken on the question of civil rights. In a sermon in 1966, Bishop Hall fervently admonished his churches to support civil rights for Negroes:

Yes, I state again the only difference between a Negro and a white is his skin, and he who fights to keep the land free should enjoy the freedom of the land. He pays taxes, so why should he be forbidden to vote just because he cannot read or write. . . . The reason most southern Negroes cannot read or write is because there were no schools prepared for them. I know the move the Negro leaders are now making is of God. The prayers of the colored people have come up before God, and He is going to release His colored people. Christ died for all colors.[68]

Hall was deeply moved by the assassination of Martin Luther King Jr. He believed that King would "go down in history as being the Moses of the colored people."[69] He wrote,

The Church of God mourns the death and passing of Martin Luther King. . . . In the Kingdom of God, there is neither male nor female . . . black nor white, red nor brown. . . . To the Christian who has enmity and animosity in his heart against the Negro, I have only one

67. *Ibid.*
68. "Integration and the Bible" (mimeographed sermon, October 1966) , pp. 4–5
69. "The Shot Heard Around the World," *The Vision Speaks,* XI (May 1968) , 4.

thing to say—he has not yet truly found the love of God as he should.[70]

Chief Bishop Hall urged his followers to embrace the cause for which King died:

Dr. King fought for the freedom and recognition of his people. One cannot be a true Christian . . . and yet have a feeling that the colored man is inferior to him. When a man is not allowed to eat in a restaurant, drink at a water fountain, use rest room facilities, or ride in a certain part of any public transportation because of the color of his skin, you may rest assured that this is a measure of slavery and partiality with which God is not pleased.[71]

In a few small white sects in the South racial justice was a major religious issue. The International Ministerial Association, Incorporated of Houston, Texas, a "Jesus only" pentecostal mission association, demanded that its members "get involved" in solving the problems of "social injustice" in the nation's black communities.[72] A similar organization with headquarters in Dallas, Texas, Life in the Spirit, in 1969 sent a team of young volunteers into several northern black ghettos to do social work. The mission was an effort to close the "credibility gap" caused in the black communities by the hypocrisy of "conventional Christianity."[73] The United Christian Ministerial Associ-

70. *Ibid.*

71. *Ibid.*

72. Thomas Black, "Let's Get Involved," *Herald of Truth*, XXV (March 1969) , 14.

73. [G. L. Munson], "Brooklyn—An Impossible Mission?" *Life in the Spirit*, VII (June 1969) , 2.

ation, an independent pentecostal mission movement with headquarters in Cleveland, Tennessee, included the following plank in its statement of purpose:

> The United Christian Ministerial Association is a religious organization seeking to bring unity of spirit to all people of all races and all churches. . . .
> The United Christian Ministerial Association does not believe in a master race but we do believe in a MASTER of all races. . . . We do not feel that economic, racial, educational, or political status has anything to do with one's salvation.
>
> . . . .
>
> 4. To seek to promote Christian Brotherhood among all races, making no difference whatever, in Christian Faith, as to race, color, or national origin.[74]

A wide variety of individuals in the southern sectarian community supported integrationist views. A few independent Baptist evangelists fought against the strong racist tide in that movement.[75] J. A. Dennis, minister of the independent Disciples of Christ Church for All People in Austin, Texas, who was pentecostal in theology, was an outspoken and vocal critic of southern racism.[76] David Terrell, minister of the New

74. "The Purposes of United Christian Ministerial Association," *Shield of Faith,* VIII (January and February 1966) , 4.

75. See [A. D. Muse], "Racial Desegregation," *The Harvester,* XIV (August 1954) , 14; Mrs. J. D. Alexander, "No Discrimination in Heaven," *Baptist Trumpet,* LXII (February 19, 1953) , 1.

76. See, for example, "Christ and the Headlines," *Texas Herald,* V (September–October 1954) , 10–11; "Resolving Racial Tensions," *Texas Herald,* VII (November–December 1956) , 7–8; "The Kingdom of Heaven," *Texas Herald,* XIII (November 1962) , 8–11.

Testament Holiness church in Greenville, South
Carolina, and widely known revivalist, sternly rebuked
the racists in his church. In 1968, Terrell, acting in
accord with a direct revelation from God, campaigned
for Richard Nixon in "forty cities" and warned the
Wallace supporters in his audiences: "I know those
who hate the colored wanted a man in office that would
please them, but God hates no one, and He is no respecter of persons. God wants what is best for everyone,
and I want what God wants."[77]

The greatest single source of racial nonconformity
in southern religious groups was the revivalism of the
cult-type faith healers of the section. Beginning in the
1940s, some of the revivalists held biracial tent revivals and almost universally offered their healing
services to both races. But during the forties the
evangelists did not seriously tamper with southern
racial custom. Usually their mixed audiences were
segregated in separate seating sections, and appeals to
blacks were much more common in the North than in
the South.[78]

During the 1950s, the faith healers divided into

77. "Pray for Nixon," *The Endtime Messenger,* no volume (February 1969), 10. See also, Tom Skinner, "Why We Must Win the
American Negro," *Pentecostal Free-Will Baptist Messenger,* XXI (October 1968), 2–3, 7.

78. See the stories on the faith healers' revivals in the *Voice of
Healing* beginning in 1948. There were some individual differences in
the revivalists, but most of them followed similar patterns until the
mid-1950s. The most southern integrated audience shown in the
Voice of Healing before 1950 was in Baltimore. See "Over 1100 Seek
Salvation in Nankivell Campaign in Baltimore," *Voice of Healing,*
II (November 1949), 3.

moderate and radical wings; this division was obvious
not only in the theology of the evangelists and their
relations with the organized sects but also in their
racial behavior. The moderate revivalists, especially
those with close relations with the larger pentecostal
sects, were more cautious about southern racial sensitivities. The more radical faith healers of the South
seldom made frontal assaults on southern racial custom,
but they were frequently erratic and nonconformist in
their conduct.

Typical of the behavior of the moderates was the
course of Oral Roberts. Roberts ministered to blacks
from the beginning of his public ministry; by the mid-
1950s Negroes constituted a sizable part of his revival
clientele.[79] On the other hand, Roberts was no social
crusader. He carefully reported to his American
audiences in 1956 that in a recent revival in South
Africa he had respected the "color line" which was
"sharply drawn" by the Christians there.[80] The Roberts
philosophy of the 1950s was summed up well when a
reader of his *Abundant Life* magazine asked, "How do
you stand on the question of segregation or integration
of the races?" He answered, "I am a minister of the
gospel, not a politician. If you attend my campaigns,
you know that my ministry is for all people of all
churches and all races."[81] The revivalist's liberal critics

79. See, for instance, "A Few of the 4,000 Who Came to be Saved in
St. Louis," *Healing,* X (February 1956) , 18.
80. "Great Moments of the Last Great Day of the Campaign,"
America's Healing Magazine, IX (March 1955) , 16.
81. "Oral Roberts Answers Your Questions," *Abundant Life,* X
(December 1956) , 11.

were quick to point out that he "preaches a salvation largely divorced from any social ethic."[82]

Oral Roberts's racial stance has changed little since the mid-1950s. His organization is integrated, and there is some emphasis on the importance of working with blacks,[83] but when faced with the theoretical ethical problem of racial injustice, Roberts has consistently reacted with typical sectarian other-worldliness. In 1967 he repeated his earlier policy of noninvolvement: "I don't dabble in politics—I just preach the Gospel and win souls."[84] When a campaign in Detroit in 1967 brought the faith healer face to face with racial violence, Roberts urged "forgiveness" on the part of both blacks and whites and closed his appeal with a prayer that "a great revival may be given before it is too late."[85]

Some of the more radical healers have long been more deeply involved in black evangelism than has Oral Roberts. Jack Coe held heavily integrated faith-

82. W. E. Mann, "What About Oral Roberts?" *Christian Century,* LXXIII (September 5, 1956), 1019.

83. Evidence of this emphasis is plentiful in *Abundant Life.* See, for instance, "New Testament Times in Norfolk," *Abundant Life,* XX (October 1966), 4–11.

84. "A Special Message to My Partners," *Abundant Life,* XXI (May 1967), 29.

85. "Before the Storm," *Abundant Life,* XXI (November 1967), 27–28. Another good example of a faith healer with a moderate approach is T. L. Lowery of Cleveland, Tennessee. Lowery's revivals are conspicuously all white. He has close institutional ties to the Church of God and such connections usually demand more orthodox racial behavior. See *World Revival* for coverage of Lowery's campaigns. A typical all white audience in a southern town is pictured in "Alma, Ga.," *World Revival,* VIII (October 1964), 14.

healing revivals in southern cities in the early 1950s.[86] Coe, who was expelled from the ministry of the Assemblies of God in 1953, did not totally disregard southern racial customs; his 1954 campaign in Birmingham, Alabama, had large mixed audiences but they were seated separately.[87] But in general he appealed to a mixed following of blacks and whites and his revivals were generally integrated.[88]

After Jack Coe's death in 1958, a number of other southern faith healers built considerable reputations working with mixed audiences in the South. By the early 1960s, such faith-healing revivalists as LeRoy Jenkins of Tampa, Florida, W. V. Grant of Dallas, Texas, and Gene Ewing of Dallas, Texas, were holding spectacularly successful integrated revivals throughout the South. They all depended on both races for financial support, and they all openly courted black followers.[89] Ewing's motto was, "Gene Ewing, preach-

86. See Norman Gordon, "Old-Fashioned Gospel Camp Meeting in Texas!" *International Healing Magazine,* III (October 1954), 11, 15.

87. See "Birmingham Pastors Acclaim Jack Coe Revival as Greatest Ever Held in Alabama!" *International Healing Magazine,* IV (June 1955), 10–11.

88. Coe's wife attempted to keep his organization in operation after his death. The "Christian school" she operated in Dallas was integrated. See, "Loving the Children of the World," *Christian Challenge,* XVIII (February 1968), 10–11.

89. See, for example, "A Portion of the Areo [sic] Wide Campaign in Virginia," *Voice of Deliverance,* I (November 1960), 1; Ray McErath, "A Good Report," *Voice of Healing,* XIII (October 1960), 10; "Faith in Action," *Voice of Deliverance,* III (May 1963), 2–3; LeRoy Jenkins, "The Harvest Is Truly Great," *Revival,* IV (January 1964), 4–5; "Gene Ewing Healing Crusade Now in Houston, Texas," *Revival Crusades,* I (October 1965), 9–10.

ing Christ, the Savior and Healer, to all People!"[90]
The most influential and most radical of the faith
healers working in the South during the late 1950s and
the 1960s was Asa A. Allen.[91] In the mid-1950s the
pattern of Allen's revivals was little different from that
of the other faith healers. He conducted integrated
campaigns (as early as 1952 in the South),[92] but was
little more outspoken on the issue than the other
revivalists of the period. But by the end of the 1950s,
Allen began to emphasize the biracial nature of his
movement. He was especially proud of breaking the
racial barrier in such southern cities as Atlanta, Little
Rock and Winston-Salem. In 1958, after a campaign in
Little Rock, Allen's promotional magazine *Miracle
Magazine* reported, "When hearts are hungry and God
is moving, there is no time for color lines!"[93] By the
early sixties, blacks were included on the Allen revival
team and his Miracle Revival Bible Training Center
was about one fourth Negro.[94]

90. "World-Wide Prayer Meeting," *Revival Crusades,* II (December 1965) , 8.

91. See Howard Elinson's fine article, "The Implications of Pente-costal Religion for Intellectualism, Politics, and Race Relations," *American Journal of Sociology,* LXX (January 1965) , 414–415.

92. See "Miracles of Healing Occur in Meeting at Louisville, Ky.," *Voice of Healing,* V (September 1952) , 12.

93. "Miracle in Black and White," *Miracle Magazine,* III (August 1958) , 10. See also, "Atlanta Campaign Culminated with the Greatest Baptismal Service Ever," *Miracle Magazine,* V (July 1960) , 11; "Miracle Revival Comes to Tobacco Land," *Miracle Magazine,* V (August 1960) , 9.

94. See "Some Thrilling Moments '64 Miracle Valley Camp Meet-ing," *Miracle Magazine,* IX (June 1964) , 6–7; "Sixth Year Opens at Miracle Revival Bible Training Center," *Miracle Magazine,* IX (Octo-ber 1963) , 15.

In a revival in 1968, Allen made an almost un-
precedented statement on the race issue. He revealed
to his audience, and to the readers of *Miracle Magazine,* a divinely inspired prophesy which he had
recently received:

I [God] say unto thee, divide not thyselves into flocks that
are segregated unto thine own call. For I say unto thee
that segregation is not the call of God. Yea, whether it be
in My Church or yea, whether it be on the street. I say
unto thee, this is a boil, yea, and a sore evil in my sight.
. . . I say unto thee, segregation shall not stand, for I the
Lord thy God shall come upon the scene and ride
speedily."[95]

Allen obviously considered racial tolerance a key issue
in his movement. An Allen worker who reported that
the revivalist was "one of ten most influential ministers in the world today" in 1969 listed among his outstanding accomplishments,

He is no doubt the first evangelist on a national and
international scale to preach integration to mixed multi-
tudes in both North and South, and be successful in inte-
grating the races in worship under his huge gospel tent. It
has been declared by leaders that the Allen Campaigns and
his preaching have done more to make all people "one"
than any other single effort in the nation or world. Believers worship, sing, shout together, and all new converts
are baptized in the huge baptistry under the tent.[96]

The racial ideas of radical religious groups in the

95. "How God Feels About Segregation," *Miracle Magazine,* VIII
(May 1968), 8.
96. Annanelle Butler, "Who Is A. A. Allen?" *Miracle Magazine,* XIV
(July 1969), 3.

South are a curious mixture. To stereotype southern
sectarianism as socially reactionary and racist is to dis-
tort the facts. If none of the sects is dominated by
middle-class liberals, few of the larger ones are without
a vocal element of racial moderates. And on the radical
fringe of southern religion is a collection of racial non-
conformists. Few of them would be classed social liberals; none is a civil rights activist, but neither are they
simply southern racists. The presence of these diverse
elements suggests some new dimensions in the study
of southern religion and southern society.

Chapter 5

RACE, RELIGION, AND CLASS
IN THE RECENT SOUTH

*I*N a recent sociological study of A. A. Allen, Howard
Elinson argued that one cannot understand sectarian reactions to social issues without an "analysis
of class differences among fundamentalist groups."[1]
The variety of racial views in the southern sectarian
community is a classic example of class influence on
religion. The diverse racial expressions of the leaders
of southern sects confirm the multiformity both of
sects and southern society.

The moderate evolution of the racial views of a portion of the southern sectarian community is consistent
with the social change that has taken place in the South
since World War II. In fact, the pervasive conservatism of the sects in the years immediately after the
war, their strident sanctification of racism, and their
insistence on slow evolutionary change all reflect the
dominant religious and cultural values of the South.
As a segment of the southern community became

---

1. Howard Elinson, "The Implications of Pentecostal Religion for
Intellectualism, Politics and Race Relations," *American Journal of
Sociology*, LXX (January 1965), 415.

aroused to racial injustice in the mid-1950s and 1960s,
so did a portion of the sectarian community. The emergence of racial moderates is just as visible among the
sects, though perhaps less widespread, as in the older
denominations. But this evolution never included
anything but the most articulate elements in southern
Protestantism. Redneck racists remained an important element in southern religious society, as did un-
predictable radical sectarians. In short, southern religious reactions to race in the recent South are simply
a part of the story of the religious and ideological
development of the section since World War II.[2]

The assumption that the southern sects represented
a social and religious unit has obscured an important
source of insight into southern society. The sects have
persistently been dismissed because they met in shacks
on the wrong side of the tracks.[3] They generally con-
ceive of themselves as churches of the "everyday working people."[4] Of course, these images are valid. Some
sects are based on bizarre and transient appeals to the
most disinherited elements of society. Others are the
strict and moralistic institutions of the working man.
But these are quite different types of religious expression in themselves, nor do they totally describe the
sectarian community.

The larger sects have become quite middle class in
many southern communities. The social impact of
World War II and the prosperity that has followed the

2. Samuel S. Hill Jr., *Southern Churches in Crisis* (New York: Holt,
Rinehart and Winston, 1967), p. 5.
3. *Ibid.*, p. 25.
4. See *Banner-Herald,* LII (March 1945), 2.

war have hastened the transition from sect to de-nomination in many southern churches. A student of the Assemblies of God recently wrote, "The war, prob-ably more than anything else, changed the social com-plexion of the people [in the Assemblies of God]. Tragically, but true, many made money out of the holocaust of war."[5] The founding of the National Association of Evangelicals in 1942 and the emergence of the "new evangelicalism" were symptoms of the growing desire for recognition and responsibility among the sects.[6] Within many of the older sects, the emphasis of church leaders turned increasingly to im-proving the image of the church, gaining accredi-tation for its schools, providing a better educated ministry and the construction of more respectable buildings. The appearance of "public relations men" in the hierarchy of many of the sects is symptomatic of the change.[7] In short, many of the southern sects by the 1960s had evolved to serve "churchlike" functions for large middle-class elements while remaining "sectlike" in function for their less sophisticated members. Of course, as the older sects have become more middle class they have lost influence among the lower classes

5. Irvin John Harrison, "A History of the Assemblies of God" (un-published Ph.D. thesis, Berkeley Baptist Divinity School, 1954), p. 295.

6. See Bruce L. Shelley, *Evangelicalism in America* (Grand Rapids: Eerdmans, 1967), pp. 85–109.

7. For some examples of this emphasis, see "Pentecost and Fanat-icism," *Pentecostal Holiness Advocate,* XLIII (May 16, 1959), 4; "Sectarianism," *Pentecostal Holiness Advocate,* XLIII (January 16, 1960), 3; C. Y. Melton, "Emmanuel College Gains Southern Associa-tion Accreditation," *Pentecostal Holiness Advocate,* LI (January 6, 1968), 3.

in the South. Liston Pope pointed out in his study of Gastonia, North Carolina, that "any denomination" which failed to meet the special needs of the mill workers was "slowly vanquished" by " 'ignorant and disreputable' preachers of the newer sects."[8]

The sociological evolution within most of the older sects is easy to trace. By 1970, the Churches of Christ were clearly divided into three theological and sociological groups. The most conservative element of the church was represented by such weekly journals as the *Gospel Guardian* and *Truth Magazine;* the most liberal segment by the *Christian Chronicle* and *Mission;* and the middle-of-the-road, which constitutes a majority of the church, by the powerful weeklies, the *Gospel Advocate* and the *Firm Foundation.* Serious theological issues are at stake in the divisions, but the lines are clearly being drawn according to sociological class. One student of the movement has recently written,

A large segment of the church of Christ is well along the path toward denominational status. The evolution that is taking place is essentially a sociological one. It is the result of the changing character of the membership of the church. The cultured element in the movement has simply begun the search for a more sophisticated type of religion.[9]

An "innovative elite," which hopes to lead the group into a more denominational status is clearly

8. Liston Pope, *Millhands and Preachers* (New Haven: Yale University Press, 1942) , pp. 114–115.

9. David Edwin Harrell Jr., *Emergence of the "Church of Christ" Denomination* (Lufkin, Texas: Gospel Guardian Company, 1967) , pp. 27–28. See also, "Rainbow Over Abilene," *Christianity Today,* XIV (March 27, 1970) , 599.

present.[10] Conflicting racial views in the Churches of Christ fit neatly into the pattern of the dividing church.

Symptoms of emerging middle-class denominational values are just as clearly present in other southern sects. In 1947, the editor of the *Cumberland Presbyterian* bemoaned the fact that his church was "crammed full, packed down, and running over with little old shabby, one-horse buildings stuck away in some cheap half-kept corners of towns and gullied hillsides." He called for the building of "some first-class Cumberland Presbyterian churches."[11] When an older preacher urged the young leaders of the church to relax the increasing emphasis on "college-bred" ministers, the editor of the *Cumberland Presbyterian* retorted, "Ignorance does not pay off any more, if it ever did."[12] The general organizational reshuffling within the sect in 1948 which brought liberal leadership into control of the group was calculated to rid the group of the "sectarian" image and to openly declare its willingness "to work with other Christians in a common cause."[13] A militant liberal in 1969 made the issue plain: "We will be a church, not a sect."[14] Of course, the liberal evolution in the

10. For a discussion of this phenomenon, see John Scanzoni, "Innovation and Constancy in the Church-Sect Typology," *American Journal of Sociology*, LXXI (November 1965), 325–327.

11. "Some First Class Churches Need to be Built," *Cumberland Presbyterian*, CXIX (October 30, 1947), 5.

12. O. A. Barber, "Against an Educational Standard for Preachers," *Cumberland Presbyterian*, CXX (August 26, 1948), 12; Ky Curry, "Why a Prepared Ministry Educationally?" *Cumberland Presbyterian*, CXX (September 9, 1948), 3.

13. "Three Presbyteries," *Cumberland Presbyterian*, CXX (November 11, 1948), 3.

14. Roy E. Blakeburn, "A Mood of Chastened Hope," *Cumberland Presbyterian*, CXLI (August 5, 1969), 11.

Cumberland Presbyterian church did not take place without resistance, a resistance that is outlined by the racial debate in the church. Many conservatives were dissatisfied with the new leadership of the church and "a few churches withdrew from the denomination in 1954."[15] In 1968, a Memphis layman clearly voiced the conservative view of the evolution of the church:

I am beginning to wonder . . . if some of our preachers are not getting too smart, or at least so smart they cannot accept the older versions of the Bible, the Confession of Faith, and the doctrine of the Cumberland Presbyterian Church that was the rock or basis of the founding of our church.[16]

All of the larger pentecostal sects have made similar transitions.[17] The evolution of Oral Roberts was typical of the growing search for social respectability by American pentecostals. The opening of Oral Roberts University in 1965, wrote an evangelical editor, "dramatizes new intellectual aspirations among some Pentecostals."[18] When Roberts joined the Methodist church, the action symbolized a much broader social phenomenon: "Roberts is doing a lot to change the image and bring

15. Thomas H. Campbell, *Good News on the Frontier* (Memphis: Frontier Press, 1965) , p. 151.

16. E. M. Hall, "Why Lose Our Identity," *Cumberland Presbyterian,* CXL (January 2, 1968) , 11. See also, Elizabeth White Sevier, "Ministers, Listen to Laymen," *Cumberland Presbyterian,* CXL (June 11, 1968) , 11.

17. Truman B. Douglass, "Ecological Changes and the Church," *Annals* of the American Academy of Political and Social Science, CCCXXXII (November 1960) , 82–84.

18. "Oral Roberts University: Tongues and Truth," *Christianity Today,* IX (September 24, 1965) , 1299.

Pentecostalism further out of the cultural backwater."[19] To many conservatives Oral Roberts's new professionally produced television series, initiated in 1969, was a final step calculated to stamp the image of middle-class respectability on pentecostalism.[20] Of course, these changes in pentecostalism caused tensions, as they did in other sectarian streams. A chagrined Assemblies of God evangelist warned in 1960, "We have some Pentecostal preachers that'll build a $150,000 structure that'll seat 150 people! It's all sticking up in the air and around the corners. They're trying to win some bigshots."[21] Expressing his contempt for the local ministerial alliance in particular and liberalism within his church in general, he continued, "I came out of that twenty-four years ago and I'm not about to go back to that dead bunch. I'm going to preach Holiness, glory to God, and fight the devil in that bunch. I'm mad at the devil that's taking people to Hell."[22]

This diversity and tension within the southern sects is simply a repetition of ever-present patterns of religious development. Groups that were incipient sects fifty years ago have evolved into highly developed sects; some have strong denominational tendencies. On the other hand, this growing sophistication has sometimes resulted in the shedding of conservative members

19. "Oral Roberts Joins the Methodists," *Christianity Today,* XII (April 12, 1968) , 706.

20. See "Oral Roberts: Rousing Return to TV," *Christianity Today,* XIII (March 28, 1968) , 608.

21. Jacob Filbert, "Wickedness—Destruction—Deliverance," *Herald of Deliverance,* X (May–June 1960) , 15.

22. *Ibid.,* 14. See also, W. E. Kidson, "Old-Fashioned vs. Modern Pentecost," *Herald of Truth,* XXII (December 1966) , 12.

who have begun new radical sectarian movements. And ever-present on the periphery are the cult leaders who recruit followers from those frustrated with the changing character of their sect.

The varied nature of southern sectarian religion and its ever-changing balance are directly related to the class structure of the section. Sociologists of religion have left little doubt that in American society there is a "parallelism between social class divisions and denominational lines."[23] The racial views of southern sectarianism are unquestionably class expressions.

In their classic study *Deep South,* Allison Davis, Burleigh B. Gardner, and Mary R. Gardner divided southern society into six social classes. People at either end of the class structure tended to lump together into large groups those at the opposite extreme; upper-class people classed all lower classes as "Po' whites," while the lower classes labeled all of the upper class as "society."[24] But more subtle differences are obvious. W. Lloyd Warner has suggested that the social classes of the South divide naturally into three groups. The three upper classes (upper upper, lower upper and upper middle) make up "the levels above the Comman Man." In their study of the class structure of American society, Warner and his colleagues concluded that these three

23. Elizabeth K. Nottingham, *Religion and Society* (Garden City, New York: Doubleday, 1954), p. 78. See also, Russell R. Dynes, "Church-Sect Typology and Socio-Economic Status," *American Sociological Review,* XX (October 1955), 555–560; Liston Pope, "Religion and Class Structure," *Annals* of the American Academy of Political and Social Science, CCLVI (March 1948), 84–91.

24. P. 65; see, pp. 59–83.

classes constituted the American aristocracy and "combined include approximately 13 per cent of the total population."[25] Warner's "Common Man level" includes the lower middle class, "clerks and other white-collar workers, small tradesmen, and a fraction of skilled workers," and the upper lower class, "poor-but-honest workers."[26] The lower lower class is "below the level of the Common Man."[27] In the South, both classes which Warner designates the "Common Man" regard the lower lower class as a "No'count lot" and "shiftless people."[28] In short, southern society may be viewed as three-layered, but not simply on the basis of upper, middle, and lower classes. More pertinent is the distinction between "society," the "Common Man" and "white trash."

The racial expressions of the southern sects can be understood only in this class context. Urbanization and demographic mobility have certainly influenced southern society since World War II and may well have changed the ratios of the classes, but a basic three-layered society remains.[29] Liston Pope discovered twenty years ago that the churches of Gaston County, North Carolina, rested on a three-class base. One can

25. W. Lloyd Warner, Marchia Meeker, and Kenneth Eells, *Social Class in America* (Chicago: Science Research Associates, 1949), p. 13.

26. *Ibid.*, pp. 13–14.

27. *Ibid.*, p. 15.

28. Allison Davis, Burleigh B. Gardner and Mary R. Gardner, *Deep South* (6th ed.; Chicago: University of Chicago Press, 1949), p. 65.

29. See David O. Moberg, *The Church as a Social Institution* (Englewood Cliffs, N.J.: Prentice-Hall, 1962), pp. 44–49; Thomas D. Clark, *The Emerging South* (2nd ed.; New York: Oxford University Press, 1968), pp. 248–270.

easily transfer to the modern South the characteristics of Pope's "uptown class," the "mill workers," and the "farmers."[30] These occupational categories may no longer be viable and would certainly vary from one community to another, but the three classes are persistent.

Within this context, the sects of the South and their racial attitudes span the three social groups in southern society. The most rigid defense of racial prejudice and custom has come from the stable and well established sects composed of successful farmers, skilled laborers, petty bourgeoise—in short, the churches of the "Common Man." Racial liberalism in the recent South has largely emanated from the new urban middle class, the more sophisticated and educated elements of southern society. Southern sects have reflected this racial moderation to the extent that they have come to include that class of southerner. The charismatic cult leaders at the other end of the religious spectrum have their greatest appeal among the social outcasts at the bottom of the southern class system. The racial message of these religious radicals, while not typically liberal, was a unique expression of that class.

The racial liberalism in the larger southern sects was a part of a general religious and social pattern in the postwar South; it indicated simply that "the churches were in tune with a growing consensus about the race problem."[31] Such southern moderates were, in a lim-

30. *Millhands and Preachers,* pp. 49–69.
31. David M. Reimers, *White Protestantism and the Negro* (New York: Oxford University Press, 1965), p. 109.

ited fashion, a part of the "new breed" of social activists in American Protestantism.[32] But, more than anything else, the social liberalism within southern sectarianism heralded the changing character of the sects. It was proof of Moberg's assertion that "the larger the membership of a denomination, the more apt it is to look with favor upon a social-action program."[33] In short, as the sects of the South became more denominational and middle class, they quite predictably assumed a more moderate and socially conscious leadership. Another recent scholar has predicted that "as the church in the South continues its rapid organizational and bureaucratic growth, one may anticipate that the problems of integration will become easier."[34]

A number of scholarly studies indicate that as religious bodies become more denominational, as their membership becomes more sophisticated, the social and political views expressed by church members become more liberal.[35] Upper-class people bring a more moderate and tolerant social conscience to their church. The

32. See Harvey Cox's discussion of the "new breed" in "The 'New Breed' in American Churches: Sources of Social Activism in American Religion," *Daedalus*, XCVII (Winter 1967) , 136–149.

33. *The Church as a Social Institution*, p. 147.

34. Elizabeth M. Eddy, "Student Perspectives on the Southern Church," *Phylon*, XXV (Winter 1964) , 380.

35. Benton Johnson has published a number of studies on this subject. See "Ascetic Protestantism and Political Preference in the Deep South," *American Journal of Sociology*, LXIX (January 1964) , 359–366; "On Church and Sect," *American Sociological Review*, XXVIII (August 1963) , 539–549; "Theology and the Position of Pastors on Public Issues," *American Sociological Review*, XXXII (June 1967) , 433–443; "Theology and Party Preference Among Protestant Clergymen," *American Sociological Review*, XXXI (April 1966) , 200–208.

racial moderation of upper-middle-class southern Protestantism fits neatly the honored southern tradition
that the "Negro's friend" is the "upper class of white
people."[36] Not threatened by economic competition
with blacks, offering reforms which do not endanger
middle-class society, the top layer of southern white
society has increasingly accepted liberal racial views.
As southern sects have aspired to higher status in southern society, they have reflected the racial liberalism of
genteel southerners. In such groups as the Churches
of Christ and the Cumberland Presbyterian church, by
1960 upward mobility had obviously influenced the
racial views of the church.

The new racial moderates in the southern sects have
been self-conscious about the social conservatism of
their heritage, as upper-middle-class southerners have
been ashamed of their racist past. The "new evangelicals" have called for a renunciation of the past: "A
sense of social responsibility, buried too long, perhaps,
under the wrong kind of conservative instincts, is rising
to the surface and demanding a place in the sun."[37]
Educated young sectarian leaders have self-consciously
searched their past to try to explain their church's rec-
ord of racial prejudice and injustice and to try to find
precedent for liberal social action.[38] They have fre-

36. See Gunnar Myrdal, *An American Dilemma* (20th anniversary
ed.; New York: Harper and Row, 1962), pp. 68–69, 466–473, 592–597,
786–788.

37. Sherwood Eliot Wirt, *The Social Conscience of the Evangelical*
(New York: Harper and Row, 1968), p. 2.

38. See, for instance, Timothy L. Smith, *Revivalism and Social Reform in Mid-Nineteenth Century America* (New York and Nashville:
Abingdon Press, 1957), and Harold Vinson Synan, "The Pentecostal

quently seized upon a mood of social experimentation in the incipient stage of the development of their sect and issued pleas for a return to the social liberalism of the primitive days. But, in truth, such precedents have little relevance in an emerging denomination. The social eccentricities of primitive sectarian expressions are peculiar to a stage of sectarian development and to the behavior of a particular social class. What such studies tend to mark is the emergence of an upper-middle-class social conscience in a sectarian community.

Most of the institutions of southern sectarianism are still controlled by the lower-middle and upper-lower classes of the "Common Man." The sectarian leaders are those "small sect, fundamentalist pastors" who "stridently support the principle of segregation on moral grounds."[39] Liston Pope concluded in his study that "the white churches of lower-income groups" were invariably "more jealous of their racial purity than . . . more affluent congregations."[40] Bigotry, as a psychological characteristic, is primarily associated with the lower-middle class[41] and this class invariably related

---

Movement in the United States." I can see some of this attitude in some of my own earlier writing on the Disciples of Christ. See, for instance, *Quest for a Christian America* (Nashville: Disciples of Christ Historical Society, 1966) , pp. 86–90.

39. Ernest Q. Campbell and Thomas F. Pettigrew, *Christians in Racial Crisis* (Washington, D.C.: Public Affairs Press, 1957) , p. viii.

40. *Millhands and Preachers,* pp. 120–121.

41. See Joel Kovel, *White Racism* (New York: Pantheon Books, 1970) , pp. 56–57. See also, Gary M. Maranell, "An Examination of Some Religious and Political Attitude Correlates of Bigotry," *Social Forces,* XLV (March 1967) , 356–362.

its bigotry to its religion.[42] Racial violence in the South has generally been associated with this class southerner.[43] Southern blacks have long considered their bitterest enemies the lower-middle-class "strainers" who seek to "raise themselves up at his [Negro's] expense."[44] In short, those who are actively seeking to gain entrance into the "superior in-group" are likely to be the most prejudiced members of society.[45] The religious leaders of this class have always "affirmed values related to the status quo"[46] and have been deeply concerned with retaining religious respectability and maintaining a socially acceptable code of morality.[47] Within the sects of the common man, writes one sociologist, there is great pressure "to avoid controversial subjects and the minister breaks this taboo only at great peril."[48] Social conformity is the price of social respectability; the common man understands this dictum both in his private life and in his church life. This "middle-class syndrome" so obvious in southern white sectarianism is the source of the sects' "distinctly conservative

42. See Gordon W. Allport, *The Nature of Prejudice* (Cambridge, Massachusetts: Addison-Wesley Pub. Co., 1954), pp. 449–453.

43. See Allison Davis, "Caste, Economy and Violence," *American Journal of Sociology*, LI (July 1945), 7–15.

44. Hortense Powdermaker, *After Freedom* (New York: The Viking Press, 1939), p. 28. See also, Myrdal, *An American Dilemma*, p. 597.

45. Allport, *The Nature of Prejudice*, pp. 452–453.

46. Moberg, *The Church as a Social Institution*, p. 137; see pp. 136–143.

47. Davis, *et al., Deep South*, pp. 75–79.

48. Joseph C. Hough Jr., *Black Power and White Protestants* (London, Oxford, and New York: Oxford University Press, 1968), p. 186; see pp. 184–188.

position in regard to racial integration."[49] Campbell and Pettigrew point out that the sectarian minister gains much from social conformity on the race issue:

By the single act of defending segregation, he secured publicity and prestige for himself, legitimized the preferences of the public majority, and effectively neutralized the denominational minister's efforts to aid the cause of integration by appealing to the Christian conscience.[50]

Benton Johnson has suggested that few American religious groups are truly sects, because few are totally opposed to their "secular environment." In fact, the groups called sects in this country generally reinforce cultural values. Johnson argues that "one of the most important functions" of such sects as the pentecostal groups has been to "socialize potentially dissident elements—particularly the lower classes—in dominant values."[51] However one may feel about the question of terminology, it is no doubt true that a large number of the sects are made up of common people and reflect the social conformity typical of that social group. A recent study of Canadian sects points out that conservative "political emphasis emerged as they [religious groups] became less sect-like . . . and became more metropolitan with commercially prosperous members."[52] The organized sects studied by Pope in Gaston County,

49. *Ibid.*, p. 187.

50. *Christians in Racial Crisis*, p. 61; see also, pp. 131–132.

51. "On Church and Sect," pp. 546–547.

52. S. D. Clark, "The Religious Sect in Canadian Politics," *American Journal of Sociology*, LI (November 1945) , 207–216. See also, Moberg, *The Church as a Social Institution*, pp. 86–87.

North Carolina, were made up of the millworker class,
not the lower-class farmers.[53] The better organized and
more visible sects do not appeal to the lowest segment
of society, nor do they reflect their views.

In short, the racism of southern sectarianism is the
racism of the common man of the South. It is typical of
southern sects, and of the older churches, in so far as
the sects are the institutions of the common people. A
liberal clergyman has proposed that these conservative
preachers are "a small and diminishing minority when
compared to the vast number of American clergymen
who stand in opposition to racial discrimination."[54]
But such estimates ignore totally the social sources of
southern religious racism, and the continuing presence
of the redneck common man.

The religious and social views of the lowest class in
southern society are reflected only in the cult leaders
and the small incipient sects of the section. Clearly
these radical religions represent those classes and castes
of our population which are socially and economically
insecure.[55] Organized religion is ineffective among the
poor whites of the South, and scholars have sometimes
assumed that the class was basically irreligious.[56] But,

53. See *Millhands and Preachers,* pp. 96–116.
54. Joseph H. Fichter, "American Religion and the Negro,"
Daedalus, XCIV (Fall 1965), 1093.
55. G. Norman Eddy, "Store-Front Religion," *Religion in Life,*
XXVIII (Winter 1958–59), 84.
56. See John Dollard, *Caste and Class in a Southern Town* (New
Haven: Yale University Press, 1937), pp. 462–463; Rodney Stark,
"Class, Radicalism and Religious Involvement in Great Britain,"
American Sociological Review, XXIX (October 1964), 688–706.

in truth, the lower class is not less religious, it is simply less attached to the religious institutions of its society.[57] Rodney Stark and Charles Y. Glock have clearly demonstrated that "religious commitment" is a "multidimensional phenomenon" which cannot be confused with church attendance.[58] N. J. Demerath III, in a study completed under Glock at the University of California's Survey Research Center, convincingly argues that the poor have deep religious commitments, in spite of their lack of interest in organized religion.[59] The disinherited simply have little interest in the religious institutions controlled by the classes above them; in most well organized sects they are clearly excluded from leadership by the more stable working classes who are their social superiors.[60] The lower class in southern society can find religious acceptance and a platform for religious expression only in the least respectable sect-and-cult forms. Thirty years ago a study of migrant cotton pickers in the South revealed that they considered the pentecostal

57. See two recent articles by Erich Goode, "Social Class and Church Participation," *American Journal of Sociology*, LXXII (July 1966), 102–111; and "Class Styles of Religious Sociation," *British Journal of Sociology*, XIX (March 1968), 1–16.

58. Rodney Stark and Charles Y. Glock, *American Piety: The Nature of Religious Commitment* (Berkeley: University of California Press, 1968), pp. 11–21.

59. See N. J. Demerath III, *Social Class in American Protestantism* (Chicago: Rand McNally, 1965).

60. Eddy, "Store-Front Religion," 71. In *The Mind of the South* (New York: A. A. Knopf, 1941), Wilbur J. Cash marked the rise of the sects as a symptom of "the rapid widening of the physical and social gulf between the classes" of the South. P. 289.

church the only "easily available form of social participation for them."[61]

The poor whites of the South are a relatively inarticulate element in the society, and, while scholars have
been interested in the class, few good sketches of lower-
class southerners exist.[62] What is obvious is that the
social behavior of the class is not typically southern.
"Flaunting of the mores" of the dominant society and
"lax behavior" have always been marks of southern
"white trash."[63] In his study of the class, Morton Rubin
discovered that they generally "opposed the mores of
the community . . . especially in the areas of economics (industry), education, drink and indulgence, sex."[64]
And, probably the most important of the deviations in
the minds of most southerners, there was a permissive
mixing of lower-class whites and blacks, especially in
illicit sex relationships.[65]

An interesting essay on "red-neck" and "pecker-
wood" culture, written by Leonard W. Doob, is included in John Dollard's *Caste and Class in a Southern
Town.* Doob discovered that lower-class southerners

61. John B. Holt, "Holiness Religion: Cultural Shock and Social
Reorganization," *American Sociological Review,* V (October 1940),
745.

62. Hortense Powdermaker commented on the difficulties of study-
ing the class. See *After Freedom,* p. xii.

63. Morton Rubin, *Plantation County* (Chapel Hill: University of
North Carolina Press, 1951), p. 111. See also, Dollard, *Caste and Class
in a Southern Town,* pp. 75–76; Warner, *et al., Social Class in
America,* pp. 17–18. For an interesting example of lower class moral
laxity, see Vance Randolph, "Nakedness in Ozark Folk Belief,"
Journal of American Folklore, LXVI (October 1953), 331–339.

64. *Plantation County,* p. 111.

65. *Ibid.,* p. 97.

were extremely class conscious and prejudiced against
the upper classes, "indecent" and "immoral" in their
conduct, and radical sectarian in their religion. The
religious independence of the poor whites, argued
Doob, was partially rooted in their hostility toward the
upper classes and the institutions which are controlled
by them. But most revealing were the racial attitudes
of the lower class southerners studied by Doob. While
they generally accepted "most of the prejudices" of
their society, "the poor white prejudice against the
Negro . . . is not strong." "Since poor whites, due to
their inferior position in society, cannot exploit the
Negro caste along economic lines," continued Doob,
"they have little of a material nature to gain from their
own caste superiority. The prestige gain from Negroes
. . . is not very great." Often poor whites conclude
that blacks "can't help it either" and tend to be sympathetic rather than aggressive in their actions toward
blacks.[66] Doob concluded, "On the whole, they have become more tolerant toward Negroes."[67]

In *Deep South,* another team of sociologists reported
precisely the same atypical behavior among southern
poor whites. They reported, "In many instances it was
noticed that lower-class whites living in Negro neigh-
borhoods treated their Negro neighbors in much the
same ways as they did their white neighbors. There
was the usual gossiping, exchange of services, and even
visiting."[68] "Neighborly relations" were the rule and

66. *Caste and Class in a Southern Town,* p. 471.
67. *Ibid.,* p. 477.
68. Davis, *et al.,* p. 50.

"lower-class whites, surprisingly enough, were sometimes friendly in their attitudes toward middle-class
Negroes."[69] Such conduct, they reported, was in
marked contrast to that of the middle-class southern
whites who "never developed neighborly relations and
were generally antagonistic" toward blacks.[70] This racial behavior on the part of the poor whites was a part
of a general pattern of "conscious, thorough disregard
for the laws of the community."[71]

Only a few of the more perceptive of the students of
southern society have diagnosed the presence of a nonconformist lower class in the South.[72] James McBride
Dabbs, in his *Southern Heritage,* astutely judged that
racial violence in the South was not basically the work
of the lower class and that the poor whites "have been
charged with a degree of racial animosity they do not
really feel."[73] Dabbs's argument is reminiscent of that of
the sociologists:

69. *Ibid.,* p. 51.
70. *Ibid.,* p. 52; see pp. 50–58.
71. *Ibid.,* p. 80.
72. Gunnar Myrdal's conclusions about lower-class southern whites
disagree sharply with those presented here. See *An American Dilemma,*
pp. 597–599. But his analysis of lower-class white racial aggressions
ignores, I believe, the personal black-white social relationship that
exists at the bottom of southern society. Lower-class hatred of blacks
is, as Myrdal points out, "displaced aggression" and does not grow
out of their natural relationships. Southern poor whites are not free
of race prejudice, and they have sometimes been an instrument of
racial violence, but none of this negates the uniqueness of their relationship with blacks. A black author who shares Myrdal's view is
Charles S. Johnson, *Growing Up in the Black Belt* (Washington, D.C.:
American Council on Education, 1941), pp. 276–284. Johnson does
note that "lower-class" Negroes and whites sometimes violated the
accepted moral code of the society, p. 278.
73. (New York: Knopf, 1958), p. 112.

There are many hints of good feeling and neighborliness between poorer whites and Negroes who live side by side. . . . Neighbors tend to be neighborly. It takes an effort on their part, or on the part of someone else, to make them otherwise. I am suggesting here that the middle- and upper-class whites, exploiting the poorer whites . . . have exercised on them sufficient influence to turn that bitterness against Negroes.[74]

It is precisely this class phenomenon which explains the racial views and conduct of the radical sects in the recent South. The flouting of social convention by radical cult leaders in the South is an expression of the social convictions of the inarticulate lower class of the section. Such religious racial experimentation may well be the only institutional reflection of these class sentiments, because the tenuous institutions of radical religion are the only social institutions controlled by the southern poor white. Of course, southern poor whites are not without racial prejudice, but they do exist in an interracial society and they do maintain with southern blacks a personal relationship peculiar to their class in southern society. They are, furthermore, indifferent to the pressure to conform. The result is a fascinating level of interracial religious communion in the South.[75]

Few scholars have noticed this level of southern religion and none has seriously attempted to explain the sects' atypical racial behavior. In his monumental study, Gunnar Myrdal noted the presence of interracial sects

74. *Ibid.*, p. 113.
75. It is interesting to note that there is markedly less black racism in lower-class Negro sects. See Gary T. Marx, "Religion: Opiate or Inspiration of Civil Rights Militancy Among Negroes?" *American Sociological Review*, XXXII (February 1967), 64–72.

in the South but dismissed them as havens for the "curious and maladjusted."[76] A study of desegregation of the churches of Des Moines, Iowa, in 1958 revealed the same racial pattern found in the South. While some of the sects in the city were belligerently racist, others were totally integrated. "Partial integration," such as existed in many of the more sophisticated denominations, was not characteristic of any of the sects of the city. The author noted, "the sect will decide to segregate or not to segregate."[77] The author speculated that integration in a sect might stem from the "small size" of the group, or "its aggressive visitation practices," or "its frequent location in mixed residential areas." But such factors in themselves contribute little to an understanding of the "contradiction" in sectarian racial behavior.[78] Segregated and integrated sects are generally quite different types of religious institutions. Different stages of sectarian development represent in turn different classes in American society, and, consequently, different racial views. Each of these expressions is different from that of upper-class denominationalism.

A recent sociological study of the A. A. Allen Revival Movement reinforces these conclusions. Howard Elinson noted that Allen's integrationist message was welcomed by many "poor southern whites who might be expected to balk" at such teaching.[79] While

76. *An American Dilemma*, p. 971, note a; p. 872, note c.

77. Lawrence K. Northwood, "Ecological and Additudinal Factors in Church Desegregation," *Social Problems*, VI (Fall 1958), 156–157.

78. *Ibid.*

79. "The Implications of Pentecostal Religion for Intellectualism, Politics, and Race Relations," 415.

Elinson offers some doctrinal explanations for the phenomenon, it is obvious that Allen simply appealed to that class of southerner who shared his racial views. As the author pointed out: "The groups most peripheral to social and economic success—lower class, poorly educated, Negro, 'white trash,' Puerto Rican—are well represented in the Allen Movement."[80]

In fact, dissatisfaction with the social institutions of society probably is as important as religious need in the process of sect creation. In *Millhands and Preachers* Liston Pope concluded,

The sect, in summary, represents a reaction, cloaked at first in purely religious guise, against both religious and economic institutions. Overtly, it is a protest against the failure of religious institutions to come to grips with the needs of marginal groups, existing unnoticed on the fringes of cultural and social organization.[81]

One can look to the radical sect not only as a source of nonconformist racial expressions but generally as a source of social discontent. In his study of the Loray strike of 1929, Pope noted that "salaried ministers of 'respectable' churches, with assured status in the prevailing culture, universally opposed the strike; a few ministers of the newer sects and a few lay preachers and ministers without churches supported the strike."[82]

80. *Ibid.*, 406.
81. P. 140.
82. *Millhands and Preachers*, p. 274; see, pp. 274–284. Many students of radical sectarianism have discovered this general association of radical preachers with the social protests of the poor. See Harrell, *Quest for a Christian America*, pp. 86–90; Smith, *Revivalism and Social Reform in Mid-Nineteenth Century America*, pp. 8–9, 148–177; George Harold Paul, "The Religious Frontier in Oklahoma: Dan T. Muse and the Pentecostal Holiness Church" (unpublished Ph.D. thesis,

Another sociologist has recently concluded, "It is this persistence of the sectarian spirit in religious organization which has given religion its dynamic force in society."[83] This dynamic inheres in the ever-present social discontent of the deprived.

A study of the theology of the radical sects in the South does little to clarify the sources of the churches' racial views. Theology may unravel the rhetoric of sectarian racial expression,[84] but the class structure of southern society explains its sources.[85] In fact, the racial views of southern sectarians are a classic demonstration that the "great and well-known theological issues which are so earnestly debated at top levels" are by no means "the main factors" in determining man's religious convictions.[86] Moberg summarized well the predominance of social force over theological argument:

Class-related cultural values permeate the work of Protestant, Catholic, and Jewish churches. These values are often

University of Oklahoma, 1965), pp. 30–35; Nils Bloch-Hoell, *The Pentecostal Movement* (Norway: Universitetsforlaget, 1964), pp. 18–60. A recent article which forcefully makes this point is Herbert G. Gutman, "Protestantism and the American Labor Movement," *American Historical Review*, LXXII (October 1966), 74–101.

83. Clark, "The Religious Sect in Canadian Politics," 216.

84. Religious history, writes Henry F. May, gives "a knowledge of the mode, even the language, in which most Americans, during most of American history, did their thinking about human nature and destiny." See May's article, "The Recovery of American Religious History," *American Historical Review*, LXX (October 1964), 79–92.

85. David O. Moberg writes: "Social and regional differences often override theological considerations in the practical applications of Christian doctrine." *The Church as a Social Institution*, pp. 60–61.

86. Elmer T. Clark, "Non-Theological Factors in Religious Diversity," *Ecumenical Review*, III (July 1951), 355.

contradictory to doctrines which the church purports to uphold. . . . Cliques in church groups and members' attitudes toward politico-economic issues typically reflect socioeconomic considerations much more than religious values.[87]

Russell R. Dynes asserts that the members of class churches will almost certainly reflect the "characteristic traits of that level, regardless of the specific doctrinal emphasis."[88] Racial disagreements in the southern sectarian community occur along class lines, not along theological lines.[89]

In short, the racial views of southern sects, as those of other religious groups, "reflect the larger society."[90] David Reimers's judgment of the old denominations is just as applicable to the sects: "But Protestantism's treatment of the Negro was no better and no worse than that of American society as a whole. Fundamental to an understanding of the race problem in Protestantism is the fact the churches are social institutions that are shaped by the culture in which they exist."[91] Robert Moats Miller, in his essay on "Southern White Protes-

87. *The Church as a Social Institution,* pp. 459–460.

88. "Church-Sect Typology and Socio-Economic Status," *American Sociological Review,* XX (October 1955,) 560.

89. *Ibid.,* 555–560. Religion as a social force, concludes Erich Goode, "follows, it does not lead." "Class Styles of Religious Sociation," 13. Theology is more related to psychology than to class structure. For an interesting study which explores this idea, see William W. Wood, *Culture and Personality Aspects of the Pentecostal Holiness Religion* (The Hague and Paris: Mouton, 1965) , pp. 97–112. Wood concludes that the Pentecostal Holiness church attracts a homogeneous psychological group and predicts that other sects, with differing theological emphases, would also prove to be psychologically uniform.

90. Moberg, *The Church as a Social Institution,* p. 453.

91. *White Protestantism and the Negro,* p. 180; see pp. 180–189.

tantism and the Negro," concluded that the churches of
the section had "always been more Southern than
Protestant, more secular than sacred."[92] Finally, as one
other scholar puts it: "The churches are culturally im-
prisoned, that is, the practices of the church with respect to segregation and integration are greatly determined by the prevailing group norms in the area
where the church is located."[93]

Such an understanding of the nature of southern
religion, and its racial messages, is essential to a proper
understanding of southern society. An alarmed liberal
minister, viewing the rapid statistical growth of the
sects, recently warned that the "old-line denominations" would ultimately be overtaken by "Holiness and
Pentecostal sects." Since all such sects viewed social
action as a "waste of time," the end result would be a
"diminution in the over-all effectiveness of Protestant
churches as social critics."[94] But such apprehension is
based on a number of faulty assumptions. It assumes
that urbane and crusading ministers in the "old-line
denominations" have been bravely dragging an unwill-
ing South into the twentieth century. There is a heroic
dimension in imagining that the religious racial liberals of the recent South are the voices of new-found consciences and theological insights. But, in truth, they are
the theological voice of a growing moderate religious
middle-class community in the South; their success has

92. Charles E. Wynes, ed., *The Negro in the South Since 1865*
(University, Alabama: University of Alabama Press, 1965) , p. 234.
93. Hough, *Black Power and White Protestants*, p. 180.
94. Murray S. Stedman Jr. *Religion and Politics in America*, (New
York: Harcourt, Brace & World, 1964) , p. 9.

been directly proportionate to the growth of that class and the changing racial values that class has espoused in the recent South.[95] The numerical growth of the sects in no way threatens that moderate social leadership, because as the sects succeed among the southern middle class, socially conscious and moderate leaders emerge in the sects. The future of racial progress in the South is more dependent on class evolution in the section than the successes and failures of particular religious groups.

More provocative is the recent prediction of two outstanding sociologists of religion that "the religious beliefs which have been the bedrocks of Christian faith for nearly ten millennia are on the way out" and that "this may well be the dawn of a post-Christian era."[96] Rodney Stark and Charles Y. Glock persuasively argue that the proportion of liberal religion to conservative has increased sharply in recent years; the result has been a corresponding decrease in "religious commitment."[97] This observation no doubt explains the proportional rise of racial liberalism in the churches of the South since World War II. But does the change not remain one of proportion, a change in the relative size of the classes of the South? Affluence and education have changed the South dramatically, but it is not a classless society, and since it is not the sects remain vital social and religious institutions. Deprivation continues to father those fervent religious expressions common to

95. See Pope, *Millhands and Preachers,* pp. 114–116.
96. Stark and Glock, *American Piety,* p. 205.
97. *Ibid.,* see pp. 204–224.

the Christian faith for centuries. Of course, Christian faith could die, but can religious need vanish while social deprivation remains?[98]

The student who would understand southern society must study southern religion; the southern religionist who would understand his church must examine southern society. With rare insight, Liston Pope wrote in 1942, "It may be that the churches will not be able to overcome racial segregation significantly in their lives until they learn also to break down class lines."[99] If it happens to be true that religious groups rarely transcend class prejudices in their social pronouncements, if they are, indeed, naturally germinated for the purpose of lending sanctity to class views, then it is well to recognize the truth. And it is well to place all religiously supported social dictums on a common level of authority. And, perhaps, one may learn that the best way to manipulate the racial conscience of modern southerners is not through self-righteousness and bombast but by careful analysis of class interests and the psychology of the common man.

98. See Charles Y. Glock, "The Role of Deprivation in the Origin and Evolution of Religious Groups," in Robert Lee and Martin E. Marty, eds., *Religion and Social Conflict* (New York: Oxford University Press, 1964) , pp. 24–36.

99. *Millhands and Preachers,* p. 121. Veteran historian Elmer T. Clark also called for Christian scholars to "begin to delve into the problem of economics, temperament, church pride, personality, the deep human hungers, and the whole complex pattern of the mental make-up and social relationship of man." "Non-Theological Factors in Religious Diversity," p. 356.

BIBLIOGRAPHICAL ESSAY

By far the most fruitful single source of information about southern sectarianism since World War II is the vast amount of periodical literature which has been published. The periodicals vary greatly in quality and influence. Few collections are available to the scholar, but one can hardly appreciate the enormous diversity within the southern sectarian community without a broad sampling of this literature. The discussion that follows includes not only the more important sectarian journals in the South but also a sampling of the relatively obscure magazines which have limited circulations but are typical of a persisting type of religious mind in the section.

Within the Churches of Christ the variety of journals springs from deep internal divisions in the church. The two most important periodicals of the conservative element in the sect are the *Gospel Guardian,* 1949– , published in Lufkin, Texas; and *Truth Magazine,* 1955– , published in Orlando, Florida. Two moderate weekly papers are probably the most influential in the movement, the *Gospel Advocate,* 1855–   (Nashville, Tennessee) and the *Firm Foundation,* 1884–   (Austin, Texas). The two most important expressions of liberalism in the church are the *Christian Chronicle,* 1942–   (Abilene, Texas) and *Mission,* 1968– (Abilene, Texas). *The Voice of Freedom,* 1952–   (Nashville, Tennessee) is an interesting "nonde-

135

nominational" publication owned and edited by Churches
of Christ ministers. It is anti-Catholic and anti-Communist
in conception and has a circulation of about 18,000.

Primitive Baptist periodicals are numerous and old. Typical are the *Advocate and Messenger,* 1854– , published in
Luray, Virginia, by Albert F. Sudduth; the *Baptist Trumpet,* 1891–   (Killene, Texas) ; and *Old Faith Contender,*
1922– (Elon College, North Carolina) . Perhaps more
than any of the southern sectarian journals, the Primitive
Baptist papers eschew social subjects. This is also typical,
however, of the official publication of the Regular Baptist
church, the *Regular Baptist,* 1877– , published in Washington, D.C. Much more socially conscious is the *Free Will
Baptist,* 1885–   (Ayden, North Carolina) .

The official publication of the Cumberland Presbyterian
church is the *Cumberland Presbyterian,* 1828–   (Memphis, Tennessee) . The paper made a major liberal transition in 1948 when C. Ray Dobbins became editor.

Each of the major Pentecostal bodies of the South has an
official publication. The *Pentecostal Evangel,* 1919–   is
the weekly published in Springfield, Missouri, by the Assemblies of God. The *Church of God Evangel,* 1910–
(Cleveland, Tennessee) is the official publication of the
Church of God with headquarters in Cleveland, Tennessee.
The weekly publication of the Pentecostal Holiness church
is the *Pentecostal Holiness Advocate,* 1917–   (Franklin
Springs, Ga.) .

Most of the smaller pentecostal churches also have official journals. The *White Wing Messenger,* 1923–   (Cleveland, Tennessee) is the official organ of the Church of
God of Prophecy. *Wings of Truth,* 1937– (Roanoke, Virginia) is the sect's state paper in Virginia. The Pentecostal
Church of God of America publishes the *Pentecostal Messenger,* 1926–   in Joplin, Missouri. The Congregational
Holiness church, a splinter from the Pentecostal Holiness

church, publishes the *Gospel Messenger,* 1924– (Carroll-
ton Georgia). The *Gospel Herald,* 1940– is a monthly
published in Jellico, Tennessee, by the Church of God of
the Mountain Assembly, Inc. The official organ of the Pentecostal Free Will Baptist church is the *Pentecostal Free
Will Baptist Messenger,* 1947– (Dunn, North Carolina).
Since 1967, the Emmanuel Holiness church has published
the *Emmanuel Holiness Messenger,* in Anderson, South
Carolina.

Scores of religious groups in the South consist of no more
than a loose collection of a few churches. Many of these
microscopic groups, most of them unlisted in any catalogues
of sects, also publish "official" journals. A typical sampling
of such publications is the *Bridegroom's Messenger,* 1912–
(Atlanta, Georgia), the official publication of the International Pentecostal Assemblies; the *Apostolic Faith Messenger,* 1930– (Oak Grove, Arkansas), which is "devoted to
the interests of the Church of God, of the Apostolic Faith";
Apostolic Witness, 1952– (Myrtle, Mississippi), "the official organ of the Assemblies of the Lord Jesus Christ";
Light of the World, 1954– (Cleveland, Tennessee), publication of the Jesus church; *Midnight Cry Messenger,*
1956– (Southern Pines, North Carolina), published by
the Bible Tabernacle of Southern Pines; the official organ
of the Church of God (Jerusalem Acres), *The Vision
Speaks,* 1957– (Cleveland, Tennessee); the *Free Will
Baptist Advance,* 1958– (Camden, South Carolina), a
quarterly publication of the Free Will Baptist Churches of
the Pentecostal Faith; *The Herald,* 1964– (Drumright,
Oklahoma), published by the Church of God of the Apostolic Faith; and the *Endtime Messenger,* 1957– (Greenville, South Carolina), published by the New Testament
Holiness Church, Inc.

The independent sectarian journals of the South also
vary greatly in size and influence. Some of the independent

Baptist journals are extremely powerful; all are consistently conservative in approach. The *Fundamentalist,* edited from 1917 to 1952 by J. Frank Norris in Ft. Worth, Texas, has since been edited by Harvey H. Springer in the interest of the conservative World Baptist Fellowship. The *Baptist Bible Tribune,* 1950–   (Springfield, Missouri), is edited by Noel Smith for the Baptist Bible Fellowship. The *Orthodox Baptist,* 1930–   (Ardmore, Oklahoma), is published by the First Orthodox Baptist Church of Ardmore, Oklahoma, in the interest of "promoting truth, harmony, and fellowship among Bible-believing Baptists everywhere." Probably the most influential of the southern independent journals edited by an independent Baptist minister is the *Sword of the Lord,* 1934–   (Murfreesboro, Tennessee). Editor John R. Rice has been an important southern evangelist for more than three decades. Smaller journals expressing the conservative Baptist view are *The Harvester,* 1940–   (Louisville, Kentucky); *Baptist Faith and Missions,* 1955–   (Lebanon, Tennessee); the *Flag of Truth,* 1957–   (Ft. Worth, Texas); *Baptist Challenge,* 1960– (Little Rock, Arkansas); and the *Baptist Banner,* 1966– (Tompkinsville, Kentucky).

Other conservative preachers published independent journals which were also influential in the section. A number of conservative Christian church preachers in the Southwest edit independent journals which are circulated widely throughout the South. The *Texas Herald,* 1949–   (Austin, Texas) is published by J. A. Dennis, a pentecostal-oriented Christian church minister. Another influential conservative Christian church minister who appeals to a wide audience of sectarians in the South is A. B. McReynolds, who publishes the *Kiamichi Mission News,* 1944–   (Honobia, Oklahoma) and *Brother Mac's Weekly Report,* no dates (Brandon, Florida). Most influential of the conservative independent evangelists to come out of this tradition, of course,

is Billy James Hargis, whose *Christian Crusade,* 1948–
(Tulsa, Oklahoma) has a large circulation and offers a
good sample of his thought.

A number of nondenominational mission associations,
mostly pentecostal, publish papers in the South. The influence of some of the associations is fairly broad; others are
quite small. Typical periodicals are *Pisgah,* 1914–   (Pikeville, Tennessee), an historic pentecostal paper published
by the Pisgah Home Movement; the *Apostolic Evangel,*
1938–61 (Lakeland, Florida), organ of the International
Apostolic and Missionary Association, Inc., a small missionary fellowship centering around the personality of pentecostal evangelist C. G. Meyers; *Herald of Truth,* 1944–
(Houston, Texas), official organ of the International Ministerial Association, Inc., a "Jesus only" pentecostal missionary association; the *Full Gospel News,* 1964–   (Katy,
Texas), published monthly by the Full Gospel Evangelistic
Association, a small pentecostal missionary association.

Many of the evangelistic associations are no more than
corporate organizations formed by revivalists and faith
healers. The *Shield of Faith,* 1958–   (Cleveland, Tennessee), published by the United Christian Ministerial Association, Inc., is the magazine of independent revivalist,
H. Richard Hall. The *Voice of the Wilderness,* no dates
(Frederick, Oklahoma) is the publication of J. Royce
Thomason. The journal is "a fundamental publication,
published each month in behalf of the work of the Lord
and the preservation of the liberties of our United States."
Faith in Action, 1961–   (Baltimore, Maryland) is the per-
sonal publication of faith healer R. G. Hardy. Missionary
Evangelism, Inc., is the religious organization of evangelist
Richard P. Carter; its publication is *Voice of Revival,* 1962–
(Decatur, Georgia).

More important in the post–World War II period are the
publications of the major faith healers. The oldest journal

promoting their work is the *Voice of Healing,* 1948– (Shreveport, Louisiana, and Dallas, Texas). Edited by Gordon Lindsay, this journal was the most important voice of the faith healers during the late forties and the fifties. Lindsay publicized the work of every major American faith healer; the circulation of the journal ranged around 100,000. As the more successful evangelists began establishing independent organizations and printing their own promotional literature, the *Voice of Healing* became less important as a general faith-healing magazine. In the 1960s, it increasingly became the organ of Lindsay's own foreign mission interests.

By far the most successful of the independent faith healers is Oral Roberts. In 1946, Roberts began the publication of *Healing* (Tulsa, Oklahoma) to advertise his work. This official publication has undergone a number of name changes: *Healing Waters,* 1947–52; *America's Healing Magazine,* 1953–55; *Abundant Life,* 1956– . Of the vast amount of literature coming from the Roberts organization, these magazines have been his basic means of promoting his revivals and explaining his mission.

A number of other moderate faith healers publish their own magazines. Church of God evangelist T. L. Lowery publishes *World Revival,* 1956– (Cleveland, Tennessee) through the T. L. Lowery Evangelistic Association, Inc. W. V. Grant, editor of the *Voice of Deliverance,* 1961– (Dallas, Texas), organ of Health & Healing, Inc., attempts to give a broad coverage to the work of miraculous healing both in the United States and abroad.

A number of radical evangelists, often ostracized by the organized sects, have published influential and widely circulated magazines in the South. Jack Coe published the *Herald of Healing,* 1950–55 (Dallas, Texas). After Coe's death his wife continued to publish a successor magazine, *International Healing Magazine,* 1955–62 (Dallas, Texas).

In 1962, the name of the journal was changed to the *Christian Challenge,* 1962–   (Dallas, Texas) . Typical of the more recent radical faith healers' publications are *Revival,* 1960–   (Tampa, Florida) , published by the LeRoy Jenkins Evangelistic Association, Inc.; and *Revival Crusades,* 1964– (Dallas, Texas) , the magazine of faith healer Gene Ewing.

Before his death in June 1970, probably the most influential faith healer in the nation was A. A. Allen. Although Allen's headquarters were located in Miracle Valley, Arizona, he was extremely influential in the South. His monthly publication, *Miracle Magazine,* 1954–   (Miracle Valley, Arizona) , had a vast circulation and his revival crusades in southern cities were attended by thousands.

Another journal which should be consulted for general information about the conservative sects is *Christianity Today,* 1956–   (Washington, D.C.) . While the journal speaks generally for the most sophisticated segment of the conservative community, it often contains information about sectarian activities. The *Pentecostal Herald,* 1888–   (Louisville and Asbury, Kentucky) , official organ of the National Holiness Association, is also a useful source of information on southern sects.

Most of the southern sects publish minutes of their general assemblies. Such records do not generally reveal much about the racial views of the members of the sects. Where such minutes were found useful, they were cited in the text. The leaders of southern sects have written relatively few published works specifically on the race issue. A few such publications which should be noted are John R. Rice, *Negro and White* (Murfreesboro, Tennessee: Sword of the Lord Publishers, 1956) ; Paul F. Beacham, *Questions and Answers on the Scriptures and Related Subjects* (Franklin Springs, Georgia: Publishing house Pentecostal Holiness Church, 1950) ; Sherwood Eliot Wirt, *The Social Conscience of the Evangelical* (New York: Harper and Row, 1968) ;

and Billy James Hargis, *The Far Left* (Tulsa: Christian Crusade, 1964).

The best study of the racial attitudes of white Protestants is David M. Reimers, *White Protestantism and the Negro* (New York: Oxford University Press, 1965). Reimers's fine study is designed to trace the development of racial attitudes among the major denominations. An older pioneering study is Frank S. Loescher, *The Protestant Church and the Negro* (New York: Association Press, 1948). Samuel S. Hill Jr.'s *Southern Churches in Crisis* (New York: Holt, Rinehart and Winston, 1967) is a less scholarly study of the recent racial attitudes of the major southern denominations. *Black Power and White Protestants* (London, Oxford, and New York: Oxford University Press, 1968) by Joseph C. Hough Jr. contributes little new information. *Christians in Racial Crisis* (Washington, D.C.: Public Affairs Press, 1959) by Ernest Q. Campbell and Thomas F. Pettigrew is a revealing study of religion and race in Little Rock, Arkansas. It is particularly pertinent to this study. An important article by the same authors is "Men and God in Racial Crisis," *Christian Century*, LXXV (June 4, 1958), 663. Another interesting article is Robert Moats Miller, "Southern White Protestantism and the Negro," in Charles E. Wynes, ed., *The Negro in the South Since 1865* (University, Alabama: University of Alabama Press, 1965). A broadly interpretative article is Joseph H. Fichter, "American Religion and the Negro," *Daedalus*, XCIV (Fall 1965), 1085–1106.

Studies of racial attitudes within a denomination are rare. Dwight W. Culver's *Negro Segregation in the Methodist Church* (New Haven: Yale University Press, 1953) covers only to 1947. Andrew E. Murray's *Presbyterians and the Negro* (Philadelphia: Presbyterian Historical Society, 1966) surveys that church. A survey of southern Baptist racial thought may be found in Davis C. Hill, "Southern Baptist

Thought and Action in Race Relations, 1940–1950" (Th.D. thesis, Southern Baptist Theological Seminary, 1952).

A number of general works on American religion shed some light on racial attitudes in southern churches. Kenneth K. Bailey's *Southern White Protestantism in the Twentieth Century* (New York: Harper and Row, 1964) is a good general survey of the development of the major denominations in the South. Other general works with some useful insights are Harvey Cox, "The 'New Breed' in American Churches: Sources of Social Activism in American Religion," *Daedalus*, XCVI (Winter 1967), 135–150; William Warren Sweet, *Amercian Culture and Religion* (Dallas: Southern Methodist University Press, 1951); Murray S. Stedman Jr., *Religion and Politics in America* (New York: Harcourt, Brace & World, 1964); Sidney E. Mead, *The Lively Experiment: the Shaping of Christianity in America* (New York: Harper and Row, 1963); H. Shelton Smith, Robert T. Handy and Lefferts A. Loetscher, *American Christianity* (2 vols.; New York: Scribners, 1960–1963); Jerald C. Brauer, ed., *Reinterpretation in American Church History* (Chicago: University of Chicago Press, 1968); Edwin Scott Gaustad, *A Religious History of America* (New York: Harper and Row, 1966).

Little of scholarly value has been published about the minor sects. The most reliable source of statistical information is Lauris B. Whitman, ed., *Yearbook of American Churches* (New York: Council Press, 1969). Some useful statistical information may be found in National Council of the Churches of Christ in the U.S.A., Bureau of Research and Survey, *Churches and Church Membership in the United States* (New York: Govt. Print. Office, 1956–58). A statistical analysis of the lingering sectarian pattern in a southern region may be found in Earl D. C. Brewer, "Religion and the Churches," in Thomas R. Ford, ed., *The*

Southern Appalachian Region (Lexington: University of Kentucky Press, 1962). Good discussions of religious statistical material may be found in Benson Y. Landis, "Trends in Church Membership in the United States," *Annals* of the American Academy of Political and Social Science, CCCXXXII (November 1960), 1–8; and Wilbur Zelinsky, "An Approach to the Religious Geography of the United States: Patterns of Church Membership in 1942," Association of American Geographers, *Annals,* LI (June 1961), 143.

Elmer T. Clark's *The Small Sects in America* (rev. ed.; New York and Nashville: Abingdon-Cokesbury Press, 1949) is probably still the best source for brief sketches of the minor sects. Other short essays may be found in Frank S. Mead, *Handbook of Denominations* (5th ed.; Nashville: Abingdon Press, 1970), and F. E. Mayer, *The Religious Bodies of America* (St. Louis: Concordia Publishing House, 1954). A number of major historians have written interpretive essays on American sectarianism in recent years. William G. McLoughlin's article on the sects in William G. McLoughlin and Robert N. Bellah, eds., *Religion in America* (Boston: Houghton Mifflin, 1968) is a harsh, even belligerent appraisal of all conservative groups. It is amazingly simple in approach; one should consult it for a catalogue of stereotyped assumptions about conservative religion. A more sympathetic and objective interpretation of the sectarian tradition in the United States by another major historian is Timothy L. Smith, "Historic Waves of Religious Interest in America," *Annals* of the American Academy of Political and Social Science, CCCXXXII (November 1960), 9–19. Other interpretative essays on modern American sectarianism are Horton Davies, Charles S. Braden, Charles W. Ranson, "Centrifugal Christian Sects," *Religion in Life,* XXV (Summer 1956), 323–358; Charles S. Braden, "The Sects," *Annals* of the American Academy of Political and

Social Science, CCLVI (March 1948), 53–62; Martin E. Marty, "Sects and Cults," *Annals* of the American Academy of Political and Social Science, CCCXXXII (November 1960), 125–134. A popular treatment with some expert analysis may be found in Henry P. Van Dusen, " 'Third Force' in Christendom," *Life,* XLIV (June 9, 1958), 113–122. Two works which treat the sects as they relate to conservatism in American society are Richard Hofstadter, *Anti-Intellectualism in American Life* (New York: Knopf, 1963) ; and Daniel Bell, ed., *The Radical Right* (Garden City, New York: Doubleday, 1963) .

A recent book which deals with the "new evangelicalism" in general, and the emergence of the National Association of Evangelicals in particular, is Bruce L. Shelley, *Evangelicalism in America* (Grand Rapids, Michigan: Eerdmans, 1967) .

The literature on particular sects is uneven. There is no scholarly study of the Churches of Christ. For a study of the background of the group, one may consult David Edwin Harrell Jr., "The Sectional Origins of the Churches of Christ," *Journal of Southern History,* XXX (August 1964) , 261–277. The only attempt to outline comprehensively the thought of the group in the recent period is William S. Banowsky, *The Mirror of a Movement* (Dallas: Christian Publishing Company, 1965) . For an interpretative analysis of recent developments in the Churches of Christ, see David Edwin Harrell Jr., *Emergence of the "Church of Christ" Denomination* (Lufkin, Texas: Gospel Guardian Company, 1967) .

An official history of the Cumberland Presbyterian church will soon be published. The best general survey of the church now in print is the brief *Good News on the Frontier* (Memphis: Frontier Press, 1965) , written by Thomas H. Campbell. R. Douglas Brackenridge, *Voice in the Wilder-*

ness (San Antonio: Trinity University Press, 1968) is a recent study of the Cumberland Presbyterian church in the Southwest.

Little has been written about the minor Baptist sects. A summary treatment is Arthur Hinson, "The Differences Among Baptist Groups in the United States of America" (unpublished Th.D. thesis, Southwestern Baptist Theological Seminary, 1950). An interesting study of the Free Will Baptists is B. H. Kaplan, "Structure of Adaptive Sentiments in a Lower Class Religious Group in Appalachia," *Journal of Social Issues,* XXI (January 1965), 126–141. The independent Baptist movement is discussed in Ralph Lord Roy, *Apostles of Discord* (Boston: Beacon Press, 1953). Robert L. Summer's biography of John R. Rice is another source of information about the independents, *Man Sent from God* (3rd. ed.; Murfreesboro, Tennessee: Sword of the Lord Publishers, 1965).

A number of studies of the radical right have discussed religious conservatives, particularly Billy James Hargis. In *Danger on the Right* (New York: Random House, 1964) Arnold Forster and Benjamin R. Epstein discuss both Hargis and political conservatism in the Churches of Christ. Other discussions of Hargis may be found in John Harold Redekop, *The American Far Right* (Grand Rapids, Michigan: W. B. Eerdmans Publishing Company, 1968), a rather defensive biography; and Harry and Bonaro Overstreet, *The Strange Tactics of Extremism* (New York: Norton, 1964) which is quite unsympathetic to Hargis.

The pentecostal churches have probably received more scholarly attention than any of the other southern sects. Several studies of some merit treat American pentecostalism generally. Probably the best is Nils Bloch-Hoell, *The Pentecostal Movement* (Norway: Universitetsforlaget, 1964). Other useful studies include John Thomas Nichol, *Pentecostalism* (New York: Harper and Row, 1966) and Wade E.

Horton, ed., *The Glossolalia Phenomenon* (Cleveland, Tennessee: Pathway Press, 1966).

A number of historical studies of pentecostalism emphasize one of the sectarian streams within the movement. Claude Kendrick's, *The Promise Fulfilled: A History of the Modern Pentecostal Movement* (Springfield, Missouri: Gospel Publishing House, 1961) deals largely with the Assemblies of God. Two other works on that sect are Irvine Winehouse, *The Assemblies of God* (New York: Vantage Press, 1959) and Irvin John Harrison, "A History of the Assemblies of God" (unpublished Th.D. thesis, Berkely Baptist Divinity School, 1954). Charles W. Conn's, *Like a Mighty Army* (Cleveland, Tennessee: Church of God Publishing House, 1955) is a history of the Church of God. *A. J. Tomlinson* (Cleveland, Tennessee: White Wing Publishing House, 1964) is a long biography written by the influential pentecostal preacher's secretary, Lillie Duggar. The book is a mine of undigested material on the pioneer leader of the Church of God. A study written by a Pentecostal Holiness minister which emphasizes that sect's contributions to the pentecostal movement is Harold Vinson Synan, "The Pentecostal Movement in the United States" (unpublished Ph.D. dissertation, University of Georgia, 1967).

Most of the published information on the faith healers of the post–World War II period has appeared in popular accounts of their exploits. Oral Roberts has received a major share of such publicity. For some contemporary evaluations of Roberts see "Oklahoma Faith-Healer," *Christian Century,* LXXII (June 29, 1955), 749–750; Hayes B. Jacobs, "Oral Roberts: High Priest of Faith Healing," *Harper's Magazine,* CCXXIV (February 1962), 37–43; "Deadline From God," *Time,* LXVI (July 11, 1955), 41; "Thrill of My Life," *Newsweek,* XLVI (October 24, 1955), 104; "Travail of a Healer," *Newsweek,* XLVII (March 19, 1956), 82;

"Frenzy of Faith," *Life,* LIII (August 3, 1962), 12–21. Roberts's official biography is Oral Roberts, *Oral Roberts' Life Story* (Tulsa: no publisher, 1952).

Jack Coe gained some national attention in 1956: "Coe's Cure," *Newsweek,* XLVII (February 27, 1956), 56; "Failure of Faith," *Life,* XL (March 5, 1956), 86. A popular article about Asa A. Allen is "Bro. A. A. Allen," *Look,* XXXIII (October 7, 1969), 23–31. A good scholarly study of the Allen movement may be found in Howard Elinson, "The Implications of Pentecostal Religion for Intellectualism, Politics, and Race Relations," *American Journal of Sociology,* LXX (January 1965), 403–415. Two other general articles on the faith healers of the period are "For Divine Healing," *Newsweek,* XLV (February 21, 1956), 86; and "Religious Quackery," *Time,* LXXIX (February 9, 1962), 42.

The literature on the sociology of religion is extensive. An excellent survey of the subject, which I have used as a guide, is David O. Moberg, *The Church as a Social Institution* (Englewood Cliffs: Prentice-Hall, Inc., 1962). A brief survey of the subject is Elizabeth K. Nottingham's *Religion and Society* (New York: Doubleday, 1954). *American Piety: The Nature of Religious Commitment* (Berkeley: University of California Press, 1968) by Rodney Stark and Charles Y. Glock is a fascinating recent study of the nature of religious commitment. Among the older studies, the pioneering work of Ernst Troeltsch, *The Social Teachings of the Christian Churches,* trans. Olive Wyon (2 vols.; New York: Harper and Brothers, Torchbook, 1949), is still useful. The first important sociological study of American religious history was H. Richard Niebuhr, *The Social Sources of Denominationalism* (New York: H. Holt and Company, 1929). A fine study by another pioneer in American religious sociology is Liston Pope's *Millhands and Preachers* (New Haven: Yale University Press,

1942). Another useful survey of the subject is Gerhard Lenski, *The Religious Factor* (rev. ed.; Garden City, New York: Doubleday, 1963). Several helpful articles are Benton Johnson, "On Church and Sect," *American Sociological Review*, XXVIII (August 1963), 539–549; Bryan R. Wilson, "An Analysis of Sect Development," *American Sociological Review*, XXIV (February 1959), 3–15; John Scanzoni, "Innovation and Constancy in the Church-Sect Typology," *American Journal of Sociology*, LXXI (November 1965), 320–327. A number of other studies which suggest variations of the sect-church typology are J. Milton Yinger, *Religion in the Struggle for Power* (Durham: Duke University Press, 1946); Howard Becker, *Through Values to Social Interpretation* (Durham: Duke University Press, 1950); J. Milton Yinger, ed., *Religion, Society and the Individual* (New York: Macmillan, 1957); and Joachim Wach, *Types of Religious Experience Christian and Non-Christian* (Chicago: University of Chicago Press, 1951).

Numerous studies of sectarian religion furnish insights into a study of radical religion and race. Two early articles which identified sectarian religion with lower-class status are Liston Pope, "Religion and the Class Structure," *Annals* of the American Academy of Political and Social Science, CCLVI (March 1948), 84–91; and Elmer T. Clark, "Non-Theological Factors in Religious Diversity," *Ecumenical Review*, III (July 1951), 347–356. Other articles which deal with the identification of sects with the lower class are Russell R. Dynes, "'Church-Sect Typology and Socio-Economic Status," *American Sociological Review*, XX (October 1955), 555–560; and Eric Goode, "Class Styles of Religious Sociation," *British Journal of Sociology*, XIX (March 1968), 1–16. Two articles which discuss the degree of "religious involvement" among lower-class people are Rodney Stark, "Class, Radicalism and Religious Involvement in

Great Britain," *American Sociological Review,* XXIX (October 1964), 698–706; and Erich Goode, "Social Class and Church Participation," *American Journal of Sociology,* LXXI (July 1966), 102–111. By far the most ambitious and useful study of religious affiliation and class status in the United States is N. J. Demerath III, *Social Class in American Protestantism* (Chicago: Rand McNally, 1965).

A good deal of interesting material has been written about specific characteristics of sects. Two articles which explore some exotic and antisocial sectarian traits are Vance Randolph, "Nakedness in Ozark Folk Belief," *Journal of American Folklore,* LXVI (October 1953), 333–339; and G. Norman Eddy, "Store Front Religion," *Religion in Life,* XXVIII (Winter 1958–1959), 68–85. A number of scholars have explored the relationship between sectarian religion and political behavior. An early article is S. D. Clark, "The Religious Sect in Canadian Politics," *American Journal of Sociology,* LI (November 1945), 207–216. Benton Johnson has written two more recent articles exploring the same area: "Ascetic Protestantism and Political Preference in the Deep South," *American Journal of Sociology,* LXIX (January 1964), 359–366; and "Theology and Party Preference Among Protestant Clergymen," *American Sociological Review,* XXXI (April 1966), 200–208. An interesting article which deals with the relation of religious attitudes to bigotry is Gary M. Maranell, "An Examination of Some Religious and Political Attitude Correlates of Bigotry," *Social Forces,* XLV (March 1967), 356–362.

Russell R. Dynes, in "The Consequences of Sectarianism for Social Participation," *Social Forces,* XXXV (May 1957), 331–334, explores the depth of commitment among members of sects. John B. Holt in "Holiness Religion: Cultural Shock and Social Reorganization," *American Sociological Review,* V (October 1940), 740–747 studies urbanization and its cultural shock as a source of modern radical religion. An extremely provocative essay about the social and psychological roots of sectarianism is Charles Y. Glock's brief article "The Role of Deprivation in the Origin and Evolution of Religious Groups" in Robert Lee and Martin E. Marty, eds., *Religion and Social Conflict* (New York: Oxford University Press, 1964), pp. 24–36. An intriguing analysis of one radical movement which is largely psychological in approach is William W. Wood, *Culture and Personality Aspects of the Pentecostal Holiness Religion* (The Hague and Paris: Mouton, 1965).

Little has been written specifically about radical religion and race. Gordon W. Allport discusses briefly the relation of prejudice to religion in *The Nature of Prejudice* (Cambridge, Massachusetts: Addison-Wesley Publication Company, 1954). A recent study which relates class feeling and racism is Joel Kovel, *White Racism* (New York: Pantheon Books, 1970). Two articles which touch on the subject of sectarian attitudes on race are Elizabeth M. Eddy, "Student Perspectives on the Southern Church," *Phylon,* XXV (Winter 1964), 369–381; and Benton Johnson, "Theology and the Position of Pastors on Public Issues," *American Sociological Review,* XXXII (June 1967), 433–443. An article by Gary T. Marx, "Religion: Opiate or Inspiration of Civil Rights Militancy Among Negroes?" *American Sociological Review,* XXXII (February 1967), 64–72, demonstrates that Negroes affiliated with sect-type religious groups are less racially militant. In short, they exhibit the same atypical behavior as do radical white sects. Even more pertinent is a study of desegregation in Des Moines, Iowa, by Lawrence K. Northwood, "'Ecological and Attitudinal Factors in Church Desegregation," *Social Problems,* VI (Fall 1958), 150–163. Northwood discovered precisely the same patterns of sectarian racial attitudes as those discussed in this study. Also consult the article noted earlier, "The Implications of Pentecostal Religion for Intellectualism, Politics, and Race Relations" by Howard Elinson.

There are many scholarly studies which touch on southern society, class structure and race relations in recent years. Three different approaches to these problems are W. J. Cash, *The Mind of the South* (New York: A. A. Knopf, 1941) ; Gunnar Myrdal, *An American Dilemma* (20th anniversary ed.; New York: Harper and Row, 1962) ; and Thomas D. Clark, *The Emerging South* (2nd. ed.; New York: Oxford University Press, 1968). Two nonscholarly but pertinent studies of southern society, one by a white man and one by a black, are James McBride Dabbs, *The Southern Heritage* (New York: Knopf, 1958), and Charles S. Johnson, *Growing Up in the Black Belt* (Washington, D.C.: American Council on Education, 1941).

Several books are particularly important for a study of the southern social-class structure and the religious and social characteristics of these classes. A general study is W. Lloyd Warner, Marchia Meeker, and Kenneth Eells, *Social Class in America* (Chicago: Science Research Associates, 1949). But more important for this study are four sociological studies of southern communities: Hortense Powdermaker, *After Freedom* (New York: The Viking Press, 1939) ; John Dollard, *Caste and Class in a Southern Town* (New Haven: Yale University Press, 1937) ; Allison Davis, Burleigh B. Gardner and Mary R. Gardner, *Deep South* (6th ed.; Chicago: University of Chicago Press, 1949); and Morton Rubin, *Plantation County* (Chapel Hill: University of North Carolina Press, 1951). The identification of southern "poor whites" in these studies is critical to the interpretation in this book. Two articles which give some additional insights into this class in southern society are A. N. J. Den Hollander, "The Tradition of 'Poor Whites,' " in W. T. Couch, ed., *Culture in the South* (Chapel Hill: University of North Carolina Press, 1935) , pp. 403–431; and Allison Davis, "Caste, Economy and Violence," *American Journal of Sociology,* LI (July 1945) , 7–15.

INDEX

Abilene Christian College, 81
Abilene, Texas, 81, 135
Abundant Life, 101, 140
Advocate and Messenger, 136
Alexander, J. D. Mrs., 99*n*, 75
Allen, Asa A.: discussed, 36; racial views of, 104–106; publications of, 141; literature about, 148; mentioned, 107
Allport, Gordon W., 120*n*, 151
Allstorm, Oliver, 65*n*
America's Healing Magazine, 140
Anderson, South Carolina, 137
Anderson, Tom, 61, 68, 69
Anti-Catholicism, 136
Anti-Communist: periodicals, 30–31, 138–139; agitation among sects, 66–72
Apostolic Evangel, 29, 139
Apostolic Faith Messenger, 137
Apostolic Witness, 20, 137
Ardmore, Oklahoma, 138
Asbury, Kentucky, 91, 141
Ascroft, J. Robert, 48*n*
Askew, W. F., 27*n*
Assemblies of God: discussed, 22; segregation in, 41–42; quotations concerning, 42, 46, 58, 75, 90, 113; racial liberalism in, 90; sect to denomination process in, 109, 113; publications of, 136; literature about, 147; mentioned, 18, 35

Assemblies of the Lord Jesus Christ, 18, 20, 137
Atlanta, Georgia, 137
Aultman, Donald S., 51*n*
Austin, Texas, 49, 135, 138
Ayden, North Carolina, 136

Bacon, L. Calvin, 75
Bafford, G. W., 96*n*
Bailey, Kenneth K., 6*n*
Baltimore, Maryland, 139
Banowsky, William S., 145
Baptist Banner, 139
Baptist Bible Fellowship, 138
Baptist Bible Tribune, 27, 138
Baptist Challenge, 138
Baptists sects, 22–24, 88, 89, 146. *See also* specific churches; Independent Baptist
Baptist Trumpet, 136
Barber, O. Z., 111*n*
Barrow, J. P., 61*n*
Beacham, Paul F., 60, 61*n*, 141
Becker, Howard, 12*n*, 149
Bell, Daniel, 78*n*, 145
Bellah, Robert N., 3*n*, 37*n*, 78*n*, 144
Benson, George S., 67
Berry, W. J., 49*n*
Bethel College, 86
Bible Tabernacle of Southern Pines, 137
Birmingham, Alabama, 80